CATHOLIC LENTEN DEVOTIONAL FOR 2025

Walking with Jesus

Copyright© Kristi K. Miller
All Rights Reserved.
No part of this publication may be reproduced, stored in a retrieval system, or transmitted in any form or by any means, electronic, mechanical, photocopying, recording, or otherwise, without the prior written permission of the copyright holder.

Thank You for Choosing Our Missal!

We are so grateful that you picked up the Catholic Lenten Devotional for 2025! Thank you for trusting us to help you grow closer to God this year.

We put our hearts - into creating this Lenten devotional, not just as a book, but as a guide to a richer and deeper experience of the Lenten Season.

Knowing that our devotional might be on your bedside table or used for family prayer time fills us with joy. We are honored to be a part of your faith journey!

We hope this devotional will continue to be a source of inspiration, peace, and strong faith for you and your loved ones throughout this EJaster season.

With sincere thanks,

Kristi K. Miller

A lifelong Catholic and passionate student of scripture, I have always been drawn to the beauty and depth of the Lent. This devotional was born from a desire to create a resource that would offer clear and engaging reflections, Prayers, and Challenges to help Catholics of all backgrounds connect with the Word of God on a deeper level.

Drawing on years of personal study and a love for the Catholic tradition, I have strived to make the reflections in this devotional insightful and practical, helping readers apply the timeless wisdom of scripture to their everyday lives.

My hope is that this devotional will be a faithful companion on your faith journey, enriching your understanding of the Easter and fostering a closer relationship with God.

CONTENT

WELCOME, FELLOW PILGRIMS 7

THE BENEFITS OF WALKING WITH JESUS 9

WEEK 1: THE WILDERNESS AND TEMPTATION 10
- Day 1: 11
- Facing Our Wilderness (Matthew 4:1-2) . 11
- Day 2: 13
- The Power of Fasting (Matthew 4:3-4) ... 13
- Day 3: 15
- Worshiping Only God (Matthew 4:5-7) ... 15
- Day 4: 17
- True Power and Authority (Matthew 4:8-11) 17
- Day 5: 19
- Victorious Over Temptation (Matthew 4:12) 19
- Weekly Theme Reflection: Overcoming Challenges and Maintaining Faith 21

WEEK 2: THE CALL AND EARLY MINISTRY 23
- Day 6: 24
- Following the Call (Matthew 4:18-22) 24
- Day 7: 26
- The Power of Words (Matthew 4:23-25) 26
- Day 8: 28
- Responding to Faith (Matthew 8:5-13) ... 28
- Day 9: 30
- The Cost of Discipleship (Matthew 8:18-22) 30
- Day 10: 32
- Stilling the Storm (Matthew 8:23-27) 32
- Weekly Theme Reflection: Answering God's Call and Facing Fear 34

WEEK 3: TEACHING AND TRANSFORMATION 36
- Day 11: 37
- The Beatitudes (Matthew 5:1-12) 37
- Day 12: 39
- Salt and Light (Matthew 5:13-16) 39
- Day 13: 41
- Fulfilling the Law (Matthew 5:17-20) 41

- Day 14: 43
- True Anger and Reconciliation (Matthew 5:21-26) 43
- Day 15: 45
- Adultery and Lust (Matthew 5:27-30) 45
- Weekly Theme Reflection: Living According to Jesus' Teachings 47

WEEK 4: LOVE, FORGIVENESS, AND PRAYER 49
- Day 16: 50
- Loving Your Enemies (Matthew 5:43-48) 50
- Day 17: 52
- Giving to the Needy (Matthew 6:1-4) 52
- Day 18: 54
- Prayer and Authenticity (Matthew 6:5-15) 54
- Day 19: 56
- Treasure in Heaven (Matthew 6:19-24) .. 56
- Day 20: 58
- Worry and Trust (Matthew 6:25-34) 58
- Weekly Theme Reflection: The Power of Love, Forgiveness, and Trust in God 60

WEEK 5: FAITH, MIRACLES, AND FOLLOWING JESUS 62
- Day 21: 63
- The Canaanite Woman's Faith (Matthew 15:21-28) 63
- Day 22: 65
- Feeding the Four Thousand (Matthew 15:32-39) 65
- Day 23: 67
- The Demand for a Sign (Matthew 16:1-4) 67
- Day 24: 69
- The Cost of Following Jesus (Matthew 16:24-28) 69
- Day 25: 71
- The Transfiguration (Matthew 17:1-8) ... 71
- Weekly Theme Reflection: Having Faith and Following Jesus' Teachings 73

WEEK 6: CONFRONTATION AND CONTROVERSY 75
- Day 26: 76
- Paying the Temple Tax (Matthew 17:24-27) 76
- Day 27: 78
- Who is the Greatest? (Matthew 18:1-4) . 78
- Day 28: 80
- Forgiveness and Reconciliation (Matthew 18:21-35) 80
- Day 29: 82
- Divorce and Remarriage (Matthew 19:3-12) 82
- Day 30: 84
- Letting the Little Children Come (Matthew 19:13-15) 84
- Weekly Theme Reflection: Facing Challenges and Standing by Jesus' Teachings 86

WEEK 7: TEACHING ON DISCIPLESHIP AND THE KINGDOM 87
- Day 31: 88
- The Rich Young Ruler (Matthew 19:16-30) 88
- Day 32: 90
- The Laborers in the Vineyard (Matthew 20:1-16) 90
- Day 33: 92
- Blind Bartimaeus Healed (Matthew 20:29) 92
- Day 34: 94
- The Parable of the Unexpected Feast (Luke 14:15-24) 94
- Day 35: 96
- Cleansing the Temple (Matthew 21:12-17) 96
- Day 36: 98
- Parables of Warning (Matthew 21-22) ... 98

HOLY WEEK: 100
- Day 37: Palm Sunday: 101
- The Triumphant Entry (Matthew 21:1-11) 101
- Day 38: Monday: 103
- The Great Commission (Matthew 28:16-20) 103
- Day 39: Whose Image? Taxes and Authority (Matthew 22:15-22) 105
- Day 40: The Weight of Choice: 107
- Judas' Betrayal (Matthew 26:14-16) 107
- Thursday: 109
- The Last Supper (Matthew 26:17-30) ... 109
- Good Friday: 111
- The Crucifixion (Matthew 27:32-66) 111
- Holy Saturday: 114
- A Day of Quiet Contemplation (Matthew 27:62-66) 114
- Easter Sunday: 116
- The Resurrection (Matthew 28:1-10) ... 116

ADDITIONAL RESOURCES: 118
- LENTEN PRACTICES AND TRADITIONS: A PERSONALIZED JOURNEY 118
- FINDING A SPIRITUAL COMMUNITY: WHERE YOU BELONG 119
- MAINTAINING YOUR FAITH BEYOND LENT: EVERYDAY INSPIRATION 119
- CLOSING PRAYER 120

Welcome, Fellow Pilgrims

A Call to Walk with Jesus in 2025

As the seasons shift and a new year unfolds, we find ourselves on the precipice of Lent, a season traditionally marked by solemnity and introspection. For many, Lent is a familiar touchstone, a time for dedicated reflection and spiritual renewal. For others, it may be a less-explored territory, a call waiting to be heeded.

Regardless of your prior experience, we warmly invite you to embark on a powerful 40-day journey—a dedicated exploration of the life and teachings of Jesus Christ, the central figure of Christianity.

Why Jesus?

In a world saturated with self-help philosophies and motivational rhetoric, why dedicate ourselves to a historical figure from millennia past? The answer lies in the enduring impact of Jesus' life and message. Jesus wasn't merely a charismatic leader; he was a revolutionary who challenged the status quo, offered radical compassion, and illuminated a path towards a more just and equitable world. His teachings, captured in the Gospels, continue to resonate across cultures and generations, offering timeless wisdom for navigating life's complexities.

Walking with Jesus transcends passive reading. It's an active journey of stepping into Jesus' world, experiencing it through his eyes. We'll delve into scripture not as a dusty relic, but as a vibrant tapestry woven with stories of love, loss, hope, and transformation. We'll unpack the lessons embedded within these narratives, considering how they might resonate with our own lives—our triumphs and struggles, our joys and sorrows.

This devotional serves as your guide.

Each day, we'll begin with a concise passage from the Bible, focusing on a key moment in Jesus' life. We'll then embark on a reflective exploration through:

- **Context:** Understanding the historical and cultural backdrop that shaped Jesus' actions.

- **Challenge:** Examining how Jesus confronted temptation, hardship, or doubt.

- **Lesson:** Identifying the core message embedded within his choices and actions.

- **Action:** Applying the lesson to your own life through a daily challenge that integrates Jesus' teachings into your world.

Throughout Lent, we'll be guided by weekly themes that connect the daily readings, providing a broader perspective on Jesus' journey. This isn't a passive experience; we encourage you to actively participate. Take time for journaling, delve deeper into the scriptures on your own, and engage in discussions with friends, family, or online communities. Shared exploration can often lead to the most profound discoveries.

The Benefits of Walking with Jesus

As you embark on this journey, you will find yourself:

- **Deepening your Faith:** Gaining a richer understanding of Jesus' teachings and their relevance to your life.

- **Finding Strength and Guidance:** Learning from Jesus' responses to adversity and drawing inspiration for your own challenges.

- **Growing Closer to God:** Strengthening your connection with the divine through reflection, prayer, and a deeper appreciation for Jesus' message.

An Invitation to All: Regardless of your background or prior experience with Jesus, we invite you to join us. This journey isn't about religious dogma or rigid rules; it's about opening your heart and mind to the transformative power of Jesus' words and actions.

Imagine the potential impact of walking alongside Jesus for 40 days. It could be a catalyst for personal growth, a source of renewed hope, or a spark that ignites a deeper connection to the divine. By the end of this pilgrimage, you will find yourself a closer to understanding yourself, experiencing more meaningful connections with others, and feeling a renewed sense of purpose in this world?

So, take a deep breath, fellow seeker. Let's cast off the burdens of the everyday and embark on this extraordinary journey together. We are confident that as we walk with Jesus, step by step, day by day, we'll discover not only the timeless wisdom of his teachings but also a deeper understanding of ourselves and the world around us. Are you ready?

Let the pilgrimage begin!

Week 1: The Wilderness and Temptation

After his baptism, Jesus wasn't whisked away to a party. Instead, he went straight to the wilderness – hot sun, wind howling (maybe both!). Why the sudden wilderness trip?

This week, we're exploring why Jesus went there and what happened. Here's the thing: while Jesus was facing the wild outside, he was also facing temptations within. We all have those voices in our heads, the ones whispering shortcuts or instant fun.

This week, we'll walk alongside Jesus as he faces these temptations. We'll see how he handled them and maybe even learn some tricks to tame our own "inner gremlins." It's like a wilderness adventure (with snacks!), but the biggest battle is inside.

So, get comfy, grab your imaginary hiking boots, and maybe a mindfulness app! This week, we're getting real about temptation and how to deal with it.

Day 1: Facing Our Wilderness (Matthew 4:1-2)

The Passage: Matthew 4:1-2 (NIV)

Then Jesus was led by the Spirit into the wilderness to be tempted by the devil. After fasting forty days and forty nights, he was then hungry.

Reflection:

Imagine the scene. Jesus, freshly baptized and brimming with the Holy Spirit, is whisked away... not to a five-star retreat, but to the wilderness. A place of stark beauty, yes, but also of isolation, harshness, and uncertainty. It's here, amidst the elements, that Jesus confronts his first challenge: temptation.

The Lesson:

The wilderness isn't just a physical location; it represents those times in life when we feel isolated, vulnerable, and tempted to stray from our path. Just like Jesus, we all face our own wildernesses – moments of hardship, doubt, or cravings that threaten to pull us off course. But here's the key: the wilderness isn't the enemy. It's the crucible where our strength is tested and our faith is refined.

Prayer:

Dear God, as I embark on this journey with you, help me recognize the wildernesses in my own life. Give me the strength to face my temptations, the wisdom to discern your will, and the courage to emerge victorious.

The Challenge:

Today, take a moment to acknowledge your own "wilderness" – a current source of temptation, a lingering doubt, or a feeling of isolation. Write it down, visualize it, or simply acknowledge it in your mind. Recognize that this wilderness isn't a dead end; it's an opportunity for growth.

Interaction

- Share your "wilderness" with a trusted friend or online community (anonymously if preferred). Discussing your struggles can be a powerful source of support.

- Find a way to connect with nature today, even if it's just a walk around the block. Immersing yourself in the natural world can provide a sense of peace and perspective.

Modern Applications:

- In today's digital age, a major "wilderness" can be social media and the constant barrage of comparison and negativity. Consider taking a social media detox or setting healthy boundaries with your online presence.

- The "wilderness" of busyness and overload is another modern challenge. If this is your struggle, consider incorporating mindfulness practices or setting aside dedicated quiet time for reflection.

Remember, facing your wilderness doesn't have to be a solitary journey. We're all in this together, walking alongside Jesus and each other. Let's support one another and emerge stronger, more resilient, and closer to God.

NOTES:

Day 2: The Power of Fasting (Matthew 4:3-4)

The Passage: Matthew 4:3-4 (NIV)

Then the tempter came to him and said, "If you are the Son of God, tell these stones to become bread." Jesus answered, "It is written: 'Man shall not live on bread alone, but on every word that comes from the mouth of God.'"

Reflection:

Yesterday, we explored the concept of the "wilderness." Today, we delve deeper into Jesus' wilderness experience, specifically his encounter with temptation. The devil, sensing Jesus' vulnerability after 40 days and nights of fasting, tempts him to turn stones into bread. But Jesus refuses, reminding himself (and us) that true sustenance comes not just from physical food, but also from God's word.

The Lesson:

Fasting, in its various forms, can be a powerful tool for spiritual growth. It's not just about denying ourselves food; it's about creating space in our lives to reconnect with God. When we remove external distractions, we become more receptive to God's voice and the subtle nudges of the Holy Spirit.

Prayer:

Almighty God, as I navigate the challenges of my own wilderness, help me find nourishment not just in physical things, but also in your word and your presence. Guide me towards healthy practices of self-denial that can deepen my connection with you.

The Challenge:

Today, consider a form of fasting that resonates with you. Maybe it's abstaining from a specific food or activity, or perhaps dedicating a specific time to prayer and scripture reading. The key is to create space in your life for a deeper connection with God.

Interaction

- Share your chosen form of fasting with a friend or online community. Knowing others are on this journey with you can provide motivation and support.

- Research different types of fasting practices. There's no one-size-fits-all approach. Find what feels right for you and your faith journey.

Modern Applications:

- In our fast-paced world, a powerful "fast" can be simply disconnecting from technology for a designated period. Put your phone away, silence notifications, and create space for uninterrupted reflection and prayer.

- Fasting doesn't have to be food-related. Consider fasting from negativity, gossip, or judgment. Choose a behavior you want to cultivate and focus on promoting that instead.

Remember, fasting isn't about punishment or self-deprivation. It's about creating space for God to fill us with his strength, guidance, and love. Let's continue this journey together, learning and growing one day at a time.

NOTES:

Day 3: Worshiping Only God (Matthew 4:5-7)

The Passage: Matthew 4:5-7 (NIV)

Then the devil took him to the holy city and had him stand on the highest point of the temple. He said to him, "If you are the Son of God, throw yourself down. For it is written: 'He will command his angels concerning you, and they will lift you up in their hands, so that you will not strike your foot against a stone.'" Jesus answered him, "It is also written: 'Do not put the Lord your God to the test.'"

Reflection:

The devil's temptations escalate. Today, he tries to manipulate Jesus' sense of faith by dangling a spectacular (and dangerous) display of divine favor. Essentially, he's saying, "Prove you're God's son by putting on a show!" But Jesus recognizes this as a trap. True faith isn't about demanding proof or seeking validation through miracles. It's about trusting God's plan and worshipping him alone.

The Lesson:

The temptation to test God or use him for our own gain is a subtle but powerful one. We may find ourselves seeking dramatic displays of God's power to solve our problems, or bargaining with him for specific outcomes. But like Jesus, we must resist the urge to put God to the test. True worship lies in trusting his will, even when we don't understand it.

Prayer:

Dear God, help me discern between genuine faith and the temptation to manipulate you for my own desires. Give me the wisdom to trust in your timing and the strength to worship you in all circumstances, even when the path seems unclear.

The Challenge:

Today, reflect on your own relationship with God. Do you sometimes find yourself bargaining or testing him? Instead, dedicate some time to genuine, unconditional worship. This could be reading scripture, singing hymns, spending time in nature, or simply sitting in quiet reflection, expressing your gratitude and devotion.

Interaction

- Share your experiences with genuine worship with a trusted friend or online community. How does worship make you feel?

- Research different forms of worship practiced by various Christian traditions. Find an approach that resonates with you and explore ways to incorporate it into your daily life.

Modern Applications:

Worship isn't confined to church services or formal prayers. Find ways to incorporate worship into your daily routine. Maybe it's listening to uplifting music on your commute, starting your day with a gratitude list, or finding beauty in the everyday moments.

Remember, worshiping only God isn't about religious dogma. It's about cultivating a deep, trusting relationship with the Divine, a relationship rooted in love, faith, and surrender. Let's continue walking alongside Jesus, learning to resist the temptations of control and embracing the power of true faith and worship.

NOTES:

Day 4: True Power and Authority (Matthew 4:8-11)

The Passage: Matthew 4:8-11 (NIV)

Again, the devil took him to a very high mountain and showed him all the kingdoms of the world and their splendor. And he said to him, "All this I will give to you, if you will bow down and worship me." Jesus said to him, "Away from me, Satan! For it is written: 'Worship the Lord your God, and serve him only.'" Then the devil left him, and behold, angels came and ministered to him.

Reflection:

The final temptation. Here, the devil offers Jesus something seemingly irresistible: dominion over the entire world! It's a promise of ultimate power, control, and worldly success. But Jesus remains steadfast in his loyalty to God. His response is clear: true power and authority come from serving God, not chasing worldly ambitions.

The Lesson:

The desire for power and control can be a powerful temptation. We may find ourselves striving for recognition, material possessions, or social influence. But Jesus reminds us that true power isn't about external validation or worldly dominion. It's about aligning ourselves with God's will and using our gifts and talents for his purposes.

Prayer:

Heavenly Father, guide me towards using my strengths and abilities in service of your will. Help me identify and resist the temptations of worldly power, and instead, empower me to be a force for good in the world.

The Challenge:

Today, take some time to reflect on your own ambitions and desires. Are they rooted in a desire for control or external validation? Instead, consider how you can use your unique talents and strengths to serve God and others. Maybe it's volunteering for a cause you care about, mentoring someone younger, or simply practicing acts of kindness in your everyday life.

Interaction

- Share your reflections on true power and authority with a friend or online community. Discuss what "serving God" means to you in practical terms.

- Research stories of individuals who have used their talents to make a positive impact on the world. This can serve as inspiration for your own journey.

Modern Applications:

In today's world, the temptation for power often manifests as career ambition or the pursuit of social media fame. Challenge yourself to reframe success as making a positive contribution, not just achieving personal notoriety.

Remember, true power isn't about dominating others. It's about using your gifts and influence to uplift, inspire, and serve. As we continue to walk with Jesus, let's resist the allure of worldly power and strive to live with purpose, compassion, and a commitment to God's will.

NOTES:

Day 5: Victorious Over Temptation (Matthew 4:12)

The Passage: Matthew 4:12 (NIV)

When Jesus heard that John had been put in prison, he withdrew to Galilee.

Reflection:

Today's passage marks a turning point. Jesus has emerged victorious from his wilderness temptations. He's faced his doubts, desires, and vulnerabilities, and through his unwavering faith, he's remained steadfast. But the news of John the Baptist's imprisonment casts a shadow. Jesus, though victorious, doesn't escape the realities of the world. There will be challenges, setbacks, and moments of grief.

The Lesson:

The Christian life isn't a one-time victory lap over temptation. It's a continuous journey of growth, resilience, and relying on God's strength. We will face moments of weakness and doubt. But like Jesus, we can emerge victorious by staying connected to God through prayer, reflection, and a commitment to his teachings.

Prayer:

Dear God, thank you for the strength and guidance you provided Jesus during his wilderness temptations. Help me remember that my own journey will have its challenges, but with your support, I can overcome them. Give me the resilience to face temptation and the wisdom to always turn back to you.

The Challenge:

Today, reflect on your own experiences with temptation. What are some situations that trigger feelings of weakness or doubt? Acknowledge these challenges, but don't dwell on them. Instead, create a plan for how you can draw closer to God during those moments. This could be memorizing a scripture verse, developing a prayer practice, or reaching out to a friend for support.

Interaction

- Share your experiences with overcoming temptation with a friend or online community. Knowing you're not alone in this struggle can be incredibly empowering.

- Discuss practical ways to stay connected to God throughout your day. This could be setting aside dedicated prayer time, incorporating mindfulness practices into your routine, or simply listening for God's voice in your daily experiences.

Modern Applications:

Temptation often comes in the form of distractions and external noise. Consider creating a "temptation-free zone" in your day. This could be a dedicated quiet time for reflection, putting your phone on silent during specific hours, or simply carving out space to be present in the moment.

Remember, Jesus' victory over temptation is an inspiration for our own journeys. By developing a strong connection with God, acknowledging our challenges, and creating a support system, we can emerge victorious over our own temptations and live a life guided by faith and purpose. As we continue this Lenten pilgrimage, let's celebrate Jesus' victory and commit to our own continuous walk with God.

NOTES:

Weekly Theme Reflection: Overcoming Challenges and Maintaining Faith

This week, we've explored the powerful themes of overcoming challenges and maintaining faith. We've encountered narratives of resilience, moments of doubt, and ultimately, the enduring strength of the human spirit intertwined with faith. As we move forward, let's delve deeper into what we've learned:

The Inevitability of Challenges

Life throws curveballs. Job losses, health struggles, broken relationships – these are just some of the hurdles we may face. While these challenges can feel overwhelming, they are a part of the human experience. This week's reflections acknowledge this reality, reminding us that we are not alone in our struggles.

Finding Strength Within

The stories we encountered highlighted the inner strength that resides within each of us. Whether it's drawing on faith, leaning on loved ones, or simply summoning our own internal fortitude, we all possess the capacity to overcome adversity. Reflect on moments in your own life when you've navigated challenges – what resources and strengths did you tap into?

The Power of Faith

For many, faith plays a crucial role in navigating difficulties. Faith can provide a sense of purpose, comfort during dark times, and the belief that there is something greater than ourselves at work. This week, we explored how faith manifests in different ways, offering a source of strength and resilience.

Maintaining Faith: A Journey, Not a Destination

Maintaining faith isn't always easy. Doubt and questioning are natural parts of the journey. This week's narratives offered reminders that even strong faith can be tested. The key is to acknowledge these doubts, seek support if needed, and hold onto the core values that sustain your faith.

Beyond This Week: Applying the Lessons Learned

As we move forward, let's carry the lessons of this week with us:

- **Acknowledge Your Strength:** Recognize the inner resilience you possess and the ways you've overcome challenges in the past. This self-awareness will empower you to face future difficulties.

- **Nurture Your Faith:** Whether through prayer, meditation, or simply connecting with your values, find ways to nourish your faith in whatever form it takes for you.

- **Build a Support System:** Surround yourself with people who believe in you and offer unwavering support during tough times.

- **Embrace the Journey:** Life is a journey filled with both peaks and valleys. Accept the challenges as opportunities for growth and transformation.

Remember: You are not alone. We all face challenges, and we all have the capacity to overcome them. By drawing on the strength within ourselves, nurturing our faith, and leaning on our support systems, we can navigate even the most difficult times and emerge stronger on the other side.

NOTES:_____

Week 2: The Call and Early Ministry

Day 6: Following the Call (Matthew 4:18-22)

The Passage: Matthew 4:18-22 (NIV)

As Jesus was walking beside the Sea of Galilee, he saw two brothers, Simon called Peter, and Andrew his brother, casting a net into the lake, for they were fishermen. And he said to them, "Follow me, and I will make you fish for people." Immediately they left their nets and followed him. And going on from there, he saw two other brothers, James the son of Zebedee and John his brother, in a boat with their father, Zebedee, mending their nets, and he called them. Immediately they left the boat and their father, and followed him.

Reflection:

Today's passage marks a significant shift. Jesus, having emerged victorious from the wilderness, embarks on his ministry. And the first step? Calling his disciples. These ordinary fishermen, amidst their daily routines, are presented with an extraordinary proposition: to follow Jesus. And their response? Immediate and unwavering. They leave behind their nets, their livelihoods, and their comfort zones to embark on a new and uncertain path.

The Lesson:

Following Jesus isn't always about grand gestures or dramatic life changes. Sometimes, it's about a quiet shift in our priorities, a decision to live our lives according to his teachings. It can be as simple as choosing kindness over anger, forgiveness over resentment, or generosity over self-interest. The call to follow Jesus is a continuous one, inviting us to integrate his message into every aspect of our lives.

Prayer:

Dear God, help me recognize your call in my daily life. Open my heart to opportunities to follow your will, even if it means stepping outside my comfort zone. Grant me the courage and commitment to live a life that reflects your teachings.

The Challenge:

Today, consider your own "call" to follow Jesus. What does that look like in your current life situation? Maybe it's dedicating more time to prayer and reflection, volunteering for a cause you care about, or treating those around you with greater compassion. Choose one small but meaningful action you can take today to follow Jesus' call.

Interaction

- Share your reflections on "following Jesus" with a friend or online community. Discuss what this concept means to you and how you strive to embody it in your daily life.

- Research the lives of Jesus' disciples. Learning about their journeys can provide inspiration for your own walk with Christ.

Modern Applications:

Following Jesus in today's world can seem daunting. But remember, it's about small, consistent choices. Maybe it's starting a daily gratitude practice, using your social media influence for good, or simply being a more patient and understanding parent. Every act of kindness, compassion, and love is a way of following Jesus' call.

Remember, the call to follow Jesus isn't a one-time event; it's a lifelong journey. The disciples, like us, weren't perfect. But they committed to following Jesus, and their lives were forever transformed. As we continue this Lenten pilgrimage, let's embrace Jesus' call, one step, one choice, one act of love at a time.

NOTES:_____
_____
_____
_____
_____
_____
_____
_____
_____
_____
_____
_____
_____
_____
_____
_____
_____
_____
_____
_____
_____
_____

Day 7: The Power of Words (Matthew 4:23-25)

The Passage: Matthew 4:23-25 (NIV)

Jesus went throughout Galilee, teaching in their synagogues, proclaiming the gospel of the kingdom, and healing every disease and sickness among the people. News about him spread all over Syria, and people brought to him all who were ill with various diseases and torments, those who were demon-possessed, those having seizures, and the paralyzed; and he healed them. Great multitudes followed him—from Galilee, and from Decapolis, and from Jerusalem, and from Judea, and from beyond the Jordan.

Reflection:

Today's passage showcases the power unleashed by Jesus' ministry. He doesn't just preach; he heals. His words aren't empty pronouncements; they carry the power to transform lives. News of his compassion and miraculous abilities spreads like wildfire, drawing people from all walks of life.

The Lesson:

Words have power. They can build up or tear down, inspire or discourage, heal or wound. Jesus reminds us of the immense impact our words can have. As followers of Christ, we're called to use our words for good: to spread the message of love, offer comfort to those in need, and speak words of encouragement and hope.

Prayer:

Dear God, help me be mindful of the power my words hold. Grant me the wisdom to choose words that uplift and inspire, that promote healing and understanding. May my words reflect your love and compassion in the world.

The Challenge:

Today, challenge yourself to use your words for good. Consider these options:

- **Write a letter of encouragement** to a friend or family member who is struggling.
- **Offer a kind compliment** to someone you encounter throughout your day.
- **Choose forgiveness over anger** in a challenging conversation.

Interaction

- Share an experience where words had a powerful impact on you, either positive or negative. Discuss the importance of using our words consciously.

- Research the concept of "nonviolent communication." This approach emphasizes empathy and understanding when using language.

Modern Applications:

In our digital age, words travel fast and far. Consider the impact of your online presence. Will your words contribute to negativity or spread kindness and compassion? Challenge yourself to use social media as a tool for good, promoting messages of love, hope, and understanding.

Remember, Jesus' ministry serves as a powerful reminder of the transformative power of words. Let's strive to use our voices to uplift, heal, and spread the message of God's love in the world. As we continue our Lenten journey, let our words be a reflection of the compassion and hope we find in Jesus' teachings.

NOTES:

Day 8: Responding to Faith (Matthew 8:5-13)

The Passage: Matthew 8:5-13 (NIV)

As Jesus entered Capernaum, a centurion came to him, pleading with him, "Lord, my servant is lying paralyzed at home, suffering terribly." Jesus said to him, "I will go and heal him." The centurion replied, "Lord, I am not worthy to have you come under my roof. But just say the word, and my servant will be healed. For I myself am a man under authority, with soldiers under me. I tell this one, 'Go,' and he goes; and that one, 'Come,' and he comes. I say to my servant, 'Do this,' and it gets done." When Jesus heard this, he was amazed and said to those who followed him, "I tell you the truth, I have not seen faith like this in all Israel! And I say to you that many will come from the east and the west and will take their seats with Abraham, Isaac and Jacob in the kingdom of heaven, but the sons of the kingdom will be thrown outside, into the outer darkness, where there will be weeping and gnashing of teeth." Then Jesus said to the centurion, "Go! Let it be done just as you believed." And his servant was healed at that very hour.

Reflection:

Today's story highlights the power of faith, even outside the traditional boundaries of Jesus' ministry. A Roman centurion, a man of authority yet humble before Jesus, approaches him with a desperate plea for his paralyzed servant. He doesn't doubt Jesus' power, but expresses his own unworthiness to have Jesus physically enter his home. Instead, he believes Jesus' word alone can heal.

The Lesson:

Jesus is impressed by the centurion's faith, a faith that transcends social status and religious background. This story reminds us that faith isn't about religious titles or rituals; it's about genuine trust and belief in Jesus' power and love. It's about the unwavering belief that even when we feel unworthy, God's grace and mercy are available to all.

Prayer:

Dear God, help me cultivate a deeper faith in you. May my trust in your power and love be unwavering, even in moments of doubt. Open my heart to see your presence in all people, regardless of background or belief.

The Challenge:

Today, reflect on your own faith. How does it manifest in your life? Is there an area where you can strengthen your trust in God? Perhaps it's letting go of self-doubt or extending compassion to someone you find difficult.

Interaction

- Share a story about a time when your faith helped you through a challenging situation.

- Discuss the concept of "universal faith." This belief recognizes the divine spark within all people, regardless of their religious affiliation.

Modern Applications:

In our diverse world, encountering people of different faiths is a common experience. Challenge yourself to see the common thread of faith that connects us all. Approach others with respect and understanding, recognizing the various ways people connect with the divine.

Remember:

The centurion's story is a powerful reminder that faith isn't about religious dogma; it's about a genuine connection with the divine. As we continue our Lenten journey, let's cultivate a faith that is open, inclusive, and rooted in love.

NOTES:_____
_____
_____
_____
_____
_____
_____
_____
_____
_____
_____
_____
_____
_____
_____
_____
_____
_____
_____
_____

Day 9: The Cost of Discipleship (Matthew 8:18-22)

The Passage: Matthew 8:18-22 (NIV)

As Jesus saw the multitudes around him, he gave instructions to cross to the other side. Then a scribe came to him and said, "Teacher, I will follow you wherever you go." Jesus replied, "Foxes have holes and birds of the air have nests, but the Son of Man has no place to lay his head." Another disciple said, "Lord, first let me go and bury my father." But Jesus told him, "Follow me, and let the dead bury their dead."

Reflection:

Today's passage delves into the demanding nature of following Jesus. Two individuals approach Jesus, expressing a desire to be his disciples. However, Jesus' response challenges their understanding of what that truly entails. He warns them that following him won't be a life of comfort and security. There may be sacrifices, uncertainties, and a commitment that supersedes worldly obligations.

The Lesson:

Following Jesus isn't a casual decision. It requires dedication, a willingness to let go of worldly attachments, and a commitment to his teachings above all else. This doesn't mean neglecting our responsibilities, but it does mean prioritizing our faith and aligning our lives with God's will.

Prayer:

Dear God, grant me the courage and clarity to understand the true cost of following you. Help me identify any attachments or priorities that hinder my commitment to your teachings. Give me the strength to prioritize my faith and live a life that reflects your will.

The Challenge:

Today, take some time to reflect on your own priorities. What holds the most importance in your life? Is there an area where you can prioritize your faith more fully? Maybe it's dedicating more time to prayer and scripture reading, becoming involved in your church community, or simply seeking opportunities to live out your faith in your daily interactions.

Interaction

- Share your reflections on the cost of discipleship with a friend or online community. Discuss what it means for you to prioritize your faith in your daily life.

- Research the lives of early Christians. Many faced persecution and hardship for their beliefs. Learning about their commitment can inspire your own walk with Christ.

Modern Applications:

The cost of discipleship in today's world might not involve physical homelessness, but it can involve standing up for your beliefs, even when it's unpopular. It might mean challenging societal norms or choosing compassion over self-interest. Consider how you can live out your faith authentically in a world that often prioritizes other values.

Remember:

Following Jesus isn't about blind obedience or abandoning all responsibilities. It's about a conscious choice to prioritize our faith and align our lives with God's will. As we continue on this Lenten journey, let's embrace the challenges and rewards that come with following Jesus, one step, one choice, one act of faith at a time.

NOTES:_____

Day 10: Stilling the Storm (Matthew 8:23-27)

The Passage: Matthew 8:23-27 (NIV)

Then he got into the boat and his disciples followed him. Suddenly a furious storm came up on the lake, so that the waves swept over the boat. But Jesus was sleeping. His disciples went and woke him, saying, "Lord, save us! We're going to drown!" He replied, "You of little faith, why are you afraid?" Then he got up and rebuked the winds and the waves, and it was completely calm. The men were amazed and asked, "What kind of man is this? Even the winds and the waves obey him!"

Reflection:

Today's story features one of Jesus' most iconic miracles: calming the storm. The disciples, seasoned fishermen, find themselves caught in a terrifying tempest. Fear grips them, and they turn to Jesus, desperate for salvation. Jesus, initially asleep amidst the chaos, awakens and calms the storm with a simple rebuke.

The Lesson:

The storm represents the challenges and uncertainties we all face in life. Sometimes, our faith feels shaky, and fear threatens to overwhelm us. Jesus reminds us that even in the midst of the storm, he is present. He offers comfort and the assurance that he can calm the "storms" within us and around us.

Prayer:

Dear God, when the storms of life threaten to engulf me, help me remember your presence. Grant me the faith to trust in your calming power, even when I feel afraid. Guide me through challenges with courage and remind me that you are always with me.

The Challenge:

Today, acknowledge the "storms" in your own life. Are you facing a period of uncertainty, fear, or anxiety? Instead of dwelling on the chaos, take a moment to connect with God. This could be through prayer, meditation, spending time in nature, or simply reflecting on scripture.

Interaction

- Share your experiences with overcoming challenges with a friend or online community. Knowing you're not alone in facing life's storms can be incredibly comforting.

- Research metaphors for faith in different cultures and religions. Many cultures use the imagery of a storm or tempest to represent challenges and the importance of faith as an anchor.

Modern Applications:

The "storms" of our modern world can take many forms: financial stress, health concerns, relationship difficulties, or simply the overwhelming feeling of being out of control. Challenge yourself to create a "calm in the storm" routine. This could be a daily meditation practice, spending time in nature, or listening to calming music. Find what helps you center yourself and connect with your inner peace.

Remember: Jesus calming the storm isn't just a story about a miraculous event; it's a reminder that God offers us peace amidst life's tempests. As we continue our Lenten journey, let's hold onto faith as our anchor, trusting that even when the seas are rough, Jesus has the power to calm the storm within.

NOTES:_____
_____
_____
_____
_____
_____
_____
_____
_____
_____
_____
_____
_____
_____
_____
_____
_____
_____
_____
_____
_____
_____
_____

Weekly Theme Reflection: Answering God's Call and Facing Fear

As we wrap up this week's theme, let's reflect on the lessons learned and how we can apply them to our own lives:

Discerning Your Call

The call to action doesn't always arrive with a booming voice or a burning bush. Sometimes, it's a quiet nudge, a persistent feeling, or a sense of unease with the status quo. This week, we explored different forms of "calls" – a ministry calling, a social justice mission, or simply a personal growth opportunity. Consider:

- What stirs your soul? What brings you a sense of purpose and fulfillment?
- Where do you see injustice or a need that resonates with you?
- Are there areas in your life where you feel a nudge to step outside your comfort zone?

Fear: A Universal Challenge

Even the most courageous individuals experience fear. Facing the unknown, stepping outside of our comfort zone, and potentially encountering rejection – these are all valid concerns. This week's reflections acknowledged the reality of fear but also offered strategies for overcoming it. Remember:

- **Fear is a natural response.** Don't let it paralyze you.
- **Acknowledge your fears.** Naming them can help you understand and manage them.
- **Take small steps forward.** Action, even small steps, can help build confidence and momentum.
- **Seek support and guidance.** Talk to trusted friends, mentors, or spiritual leaders.

Answering the Call: Taking Action

Answering the call doesn't always require a complete life overhaul. It can start with small steps:

- **Volunteer your time or skills** to a cause you care about.
- **Learn something new** to expand your knowledge and capabilities.
- **Step outside your comfort zone** by trying a new activity or speaking up for what you believe in.
- **Start a conversation** about a social injustice that needs attention.

Remember: Every action, big or small, makes a difference.

Living a Life of Purpose

By answering your call, whatever form it may take, you contribute to something larger than yourself. This week's theme reminds us that we all have the potential to make a positive impact on the world. Embrace the journey, step forward in faith, and trust that even small acts of courage can lead to something significant.

As we move forward, may the courage and faith of those who answered their calls inspire us to answer our own.

NOTES: _____

Week 3: Teaching and Transformation

Day 11: The Beatitudes (Matthew 5:1-12)

The Happiness Hack You Didn't Know Existed

Forget social media likes and the latest trends. Today, we crack open the code to real happiness with the Beatitudes (Matthew 5:1-12). These aren't your typical "eight steps to instant joy" pronouncements. Jesus flips the script on happiness, showing us it's found in unexpected places.

Reflection: Are You Happy... According to Jesus?

Close your eyes and picture happiness. What do you see? A mansion, a dream vacation, the perfect relationship? Now, let's see how Jesus defines it in the Beatitudes:

- **Blessed are the poor in spirit** (V. 3) - True happiness comes from recognizing we need God, not chasing worldly possessions.
- **Blessed are those who mourn** (V. 4) - Facing sadness and finding comfort in God allows for deeper joy.
- **Blessed are the meek** (V. 5) - Strength and gentleness, not aggression, lead to a peaceful and happy life.

The Lesson: Happiness is a Journey, Not a Destination

The Beatitudes challenge our preconceived notions of happiness. It's not about what we **have**, but who we **are** and how we **live**.

Prayer: Redefining Happiness

Dear God, help me redefine happiness on your terms. Grant me the humility, compassion, and strength to live according to your teachings.

The Challenge: The Happiness Experiment

For a week, choose one Beatitude to focus on each day. Maybe it's showing mercy (V. 7) or actively working for peace (V. 9). See how incorporating these qualities into your daily life changes your perspective on happiness.

Interaction

- **Share Your Flip:** How does your definition of happiness differ from Jesus' teachings? Discuss with a friend or online community.

- **Happiness Hacks from History:** Research historical figures known for their happiness despite hardship. What can we learn from them?

> **Modern Applications: The Beatitudes in Your World**

The Beatitudes aren't relics of the past. They apply to the pressures of modern life:

- **Social Media Blues?** Combat envy and comparison by focusing on the blessings you already have (v. 3).

- **Feeling Overwhelmed?** Practice meekness (v. 5) by taking things one step at a time and trusting in a bigger plan.

- **Stuck in a Conflict?** Be a peacemaker (v. 9) by actively seeking reconciliation and understanding.

Remember: The Beatitudes are a roadmap to a different kind of happiness — a happiness that transcends circumstances and brings lasting joy. Let's embark on this journey together!

NOTES:_____

Day 12: Salt and Light (Matthew 5:13-16)

Flavorless Faith? Not on Your Watch!

Today, we delve into Matthew 5:13-16, where Jesus uses metaphors of salt and light to describe the impact of his followers. This isn't about showing off; it's about making a positive difference in the world.

The Passage: A Scrumptious Breakdown

- (V. 13) Salt enhances flavor and preserves food. As followers of Jesus, we are called to bring out the good in the world and act as a preservative against negativity.

- (V. 13) Salt that loses its flavor is useless. In the same way, if we don't live out our faith through our actions, our impact diminishes.

- (V. 14) Light dispels darkness and guides the way. We are called to be a beacon of hope and love in a world that can often feel lost.

- (V. 14) A town on a hill is naturally visible. Our good works and Christ-like character should be evident to those around us.

- (V. 15) A lamp hidden under a bowl is pointless. We shouldn't hide our faith but let it shine brightly for others to see.

- (V. 16) Our good works are a testament to God's love. When we live with kindness and compassion, we bring glory to God.

The Lesson: It's All About Impact

Being the salt and light isn't about self-promotion. It's about using our faith to make the world a better place. Our actions speak volumes, and they have the power to inspire others and draw them closer to God.

Prayer: Lighting the Way

Dear God, help me be the salt of the earth, bringing out the good in others and preserving against negativity. Guide me to be a light that shines brightly, leading others towards your love.

The Challenge: Spice Up Your World!

This week, be intentional about living out your faith in everyday situations. Here are some ideas:

- **Offer a helping hand** to someone in need.
- **Spread kindness** with a compliment or a smile.
- **Stand up for what's right** even when it's difficult.

Interaction

- **Discuss**: How can we, as a community, better live out the call to be salt and light? Share your thoughts online or with a friend.
- **Reflect**: Think of a time when someone's actions were a positive influence in your life. How can you pay it forward?

Modern Applications: Salt and Light for the 21st Century

The message of salt and light is timeless. Here's how it applies to our modern world:

- **Social Media Impact**: Use your online presence to spread positivity and promote good causes.
- **Standing Up to Bullying**: Be a voice for the voiceless and stand against negativity online and offline.
- **Compassion in Action**: Volunteer your time or donate to causes that are important to you.

Remember:

We are all called to be the seasoning in a world that craves flavor and the light that pushes back the darkness. Let's shine brightly and make a difference!

NOTES:_____
_____
_____
_____
_____
_____
_____
_____
_____
_____
_____
_____
_____
_____
_____
_____
_____
_____
_____
_____

Day 13: Fulfilling the Law (Matthew 5:17-20)

Don't Panic, It's an Upgrade!

Today's passage in Matthew 5:17-20 might sound like Jesus is throwing out the rulebook. But fear not! He's here to explain that his teachings are not a replacement for the law, but rather an upgrade.

The Passage: Decoding the Message

- (V. 17) Jesus isn't here to erase the existing laws and teachings. He's come to bring them to their full potential.

- (V. 18) The core principles of the Law remain important. They are like the foundation upon which Jesus builds his teachings.

- (V. 19) Understanding and following the deeper meaning behind the Law is crucial. Just going through the motions isn't enough.

The Lesson: It's All About the Heart

Jesus emphasizes that true obedience comes from the heart, not just outward actions. The Law provides a framework, but Jesus calls us to a higher standard, one that focuses on love, compassion, and righteousness.

Prayer: A Heart for God's Will

Dear God, help me understand the deeper meaning behind your teachings. Grant me the wisdom to follow your will not just with my actions, but with my whole heart.

The Challenge: Digging Deeper

This week, choose one of the Ten Commandments and explore its deeper meaning. How does Jesus' teachings elevate and fulfill this commandment?

Interaction

- **Debate Time!** (Respectfully) discuss with a friend or online community: Is it possible to follow the Law without following Jesus' teachings?

- **Real-World Examples:** Think of a situation where following the spirit of the Law is more important than the letter of the Law. Share your thoughts!

Modern Applications: Beyond the Written Word

The concept of fulfilling the Law extends to our modern lives:

- **Beyond Rules:** Don't get bogged down in legalistic interpretations. Focus on the underlying principles of love, fairness, and respect.

- **Evolving with the Times:** Just as Jesus built upon existing teachings, we should be open to applying God's principles to new situations.

- **The Heart of the Matter:** In a world obsessed with appearances, remember that true righteousness comes from a heart aligned with God's will.

Remember:

God's law isn't a dusty rulebook; it's a living guide. By embracing the deeper meaning behind the Law and integrating Jesus' teachings, we can live a life that truly honors God.

NOTES:

Day 14: True Anger and Reconciliation (Matthew 5:21-26)

Beyond "Don't Get Mad": Anger Management, Jesus Style

Anger. It bubbles up, simmers beneath the surface, and sometimes explodes. Today, in Matthew 5:21-26, Jesus tackles this fiery emotion, offering a fresh perspective on anger and the importance of reconciliation.

The Passage: Decoding the Fire

- (V. 21-22) Jesus goes beyond the outward act of murder and exposes the root of the problem: anger. He highlights how anger, even seemingly harmless name-calling, can lead down a destructive path.

- (V. 23-24) Here, Jesus prioritizes reconciliation over religious rituals. Holding onto anger hinders our connection with God.

- (V. 25-26) Jesus emphasizes urgency in resolving conflict. Don't let anger fester; address it promptly to avoid further complications.

The Lesson: Extinguishing the Flames

Jesus doesn't ask us to be emotionless robots. It's okay to feel anger. But it's crucial to manage it in a healthy way.

- **Focus on the Root:** Instead of reacting in anger, try to understand the cause. Is it hurt, frustration, or fear?

- **Seek Reconciliation:** Don't let anger build walls. Open communication and forgiveness are key to repairing relationships.

- **Address It Quickly:** Don't let anger simmer. Communicate openly and seek resolution before things escalate.

Prayer: Calming the Storm Within

Dear God, help me recognize anger within myself and address it constructively. Grant me the wisdom to seek reconciliation and prioritize forgiveness in my relationships.

The Challenge: The Reconciliation Resolution

This week, choose a situation where you might hold lingering anger.

Consider taking steps towards reconciliation, even if it's simply writing a heartfelt note.

Interaction

- **Share Your Story:** Have you ever experienced the power of forgiveness? Discuss your experiences with a friend or online community.

- **Conflict Resolution Techniques:** Research healthy conflict resolution techniques. Share your findings and discuss how they can be applied in daily life.

Modern Applications: Taming the Digital Fire

Anger can flare up easily in the fast-paced world of online communication:

- **Take a Deep Breath:** Before hitting "send" on an angry email or comment, take a moment to calm down and rephrase your message.

- **Seek Clarification:** Misunderstandings can fuel anger. Try to understand the other person's perspective before jumping to conclusions.

- **Practice Empathy:** Remember, there's a real person on the other side of the screen. Approach communication with kindness and understanding.

Remember:

Anger is a natural emotion, but it doesn't have to control us. By acknowledging it, addressing its root cause, and seeking reconciliation, we can navigate anger in a healthy way and build stronger relationships.

NOTES:_____
_____
_____
_____
_____
_____
_____
_____
_____
_____
_____
_____
_____
_____
_____
_____
_____
_____
_____
_____
_____

Day 15: Adultery and Lust (Matthew 5:27-30)

Today's reflection delves into Matthew 5:27-30, where Jesus challenges the traditional understanding of adultery and steers us towards a deeper truth: purity of heart.

Reflection: Beyond the Physical Act

Jesus' words go beyond the outward act of adultery. He emphasizes that lustful desires within the heart, even if not acted upon, are a transgression. This challenges us to confront our inner world and acknowledge the power our thoughts hold.

The Lesson: Cultivating a Pure Heart

- True faithfulness isn't just about physical actions; it's about guarding our hearts and intentions.

- By acknowledging and addressing lustful desires, we prevent them from taking root and potentially leading to harmful behavior.

- Cultivating inner purity requires self-awareness, discipline, and a commitment to living according to our values.

A Prayer for Purity:

Dear God, grant me the clarity to see my thoughts and desires with honesty. Help me extinguish any flames of lust that may arise and replace them with the light of your love. Guide me towards a heart that is pure and reflects your goodness.

The Challenge: Examining Your Inner Landscape

- Spend some time in quiet reflection. Consider situations that might trigger lustful desires.

- What are some practical ways you can cultivate purity of thought in your daily life?

- Maybe it's avoiding certain media or seeking out content that uplifts and inspires you.

Interaction

- **Inner Work vs. Outer Actions:** Discuss the importance of inner purity alongside ethical behavior. How do our thoughts and intentions influence our actions?

- **Maintaining Moral Integrity:** Share strategies for overcoming temptation and staying true to your values.

- **The Power of Self-Awareness:** How can cultivating self-awareness help us navigate the complexities of human desire?

Modern Applications: Building Healthy Relationships

- Purity of heart is essential for building strong and trusting relationships.

- By cultivating inner faithfulness, we can create deeper connections based on mutual respect and emotional honesty.

- This applies to romantic relationships, friendships, and even casual interactions.

Remember:

Inner purity is a journey, not a destination. Through self-reflection, seeking guidance, and relying on faith, we can cultivate a heart that aligns with God's will and fosters healthy, fulfilling relationships.

NOTES:

Weekly Theme Reflection: Living According to Jesus' Teachings

This week, we've embarked on a journey to explore the profound teachings of Jesus. From the Sermon on the Mount to parables filled with wisdom, we've delved into the core principles that guide a life lived according to his message. As we move forward, let's gather the echoes of eternity that resonated throughout the week:

Love as the Cornerstone

Love, in all its forms – love for God, love for neighbor, love for enemy – is the foundation of Jesus' teachings. It's a radical call to compassion, forgiveness, and unconditional acceptance.

The Challenge: How can we integrate this all-encompassing love into our daily interactions? Can we challenge feelings of animosity and extend kindness even to those who challenge us?

Beyond the Material World

Jesus' teachings often focus on the impermanence of material things and the importance of seeking treasures that last. He encourages us to focus on our inner world and cultivate a connection with something greater than ourselves.

The Challenge: How can we simplify our lives and prioritize spiritual growth over material possessions? What practices can help us connect with the divine and find meaning beyond the physical world?

Inner Transformation

Jesus emphasizes the importance of inward transformation. He challenges us to forgive others, turn away from judgment, and cultivate humility. This journey of self-improvement requires constant reflection and dedication.

The Challenge: How can we cultivate greater self-awareness and identify areas for personal growth? What tools or practices can we use to tame our egos and embrace humility?

Living With Purpose

Jesus' teachings provide a framework for living a life of purpose. He encourages us to use our talents and resources to serve others and make a positive impact on the world.

The Challenge: How can we discover our unique gifts and use them to contribute to the greater good? What opportunities for service exist in our communities, and how can we get involved?

Remember:

Living according to Jesus' teachings is an ongoing process. There will be stumbles, moments of doubt, and times when we fall short. But by carrying the echoes of his message in our hearts, we can strive towards a life filled with love, compassion, and purpose.

As we move forward, may the lessons learned this week inspire us to:

- Live with more love and less judgment.
- Focus on the enduring over the fleeting.
- Embrace a journey of continuous self-improvement.
- Use our gifts to make a positive difference in the world.

May the echoes of Jesus' teachings guide our steps and illuminate the path towards a life well-lived.

NOTES:

Week 4: Love, Forgiveness, and Prayer

Day 16: Loving Your Enemies (Matthew 5:43-48)

Can You Love Your Enemy?

Today's passage in Matthew 5:43-48 throws down a challenge that might seem impossible: loving your enemies. Jesus pushes us beyond our comfort zones, urging us to embrace forgiveness and compassion even towards those who have wronged us.

The Passage: Decoding the Challenge

- (V. 43-44) Jesus dismantles the "love your neighbor, hate your enemy" mentality. He calls for a radical shift, urging us to extend love even to those who oppose us.

- (V. 45) God's love is unconditional. By mirroring his love, we become true children of God.

- (V. 46-47) Loving those who already love us is easy. Jesus challenges us to go beyond the ordinary and extend love to those who wouldn't reciprocate.

- (V. 48) This isn't a call for immediate flawlessness. It's a call for continuous growth, striving to embody God's love and forgiveness in our lives.

The Lesson: The Power of Forgiveness

Loving our enemies isn't about condoning their actions. It's about choosing love over hate, and breaking the cycle of negativity. Forgiveness is a powerful act of self-liberation; it frees us from the burden of resentment and allows us to move forward.

Prayer: An Open Heart for Forgiveness

Dear God, grant me the strength to forgive those who have hurt me. Help me see them with compassion and extend your love through me, even to my enemies.

The Challenge: The Forgiveness Experiment

This week, choose someone you find difficult to forgive. Maybe it's a family member, a friend, or even someone you don't know personally. Instead of dwelling on the hurt, try to understand their perspective. Consider writing them a letter (you don't have to send it) expressing forgiveness or simply acknowledging the pain.

Interaction

- **Share Your Struggles:** Have you ever struggled to forgive someone? Discuss your experiences with a friend or online community. How did you find the strength to move forward?

- **The Science of Forgiveness:** Research the psychological and emotional benefits of forgiveness. Share your findings and discuss how forgiveness can contribute to a happier, healthier life.

Modern Applications: Loving in a Divided World

The call to love our enemies is especially relevant in today's world:

- **Breaking the Cycle of Hate:** In a world filled with conflict, choosing forgiveness can create a ripple effect of compassion and understanding.

- **Overcoming Bias:** Challenge your own prejudices and stereotypes. Seek opportunities to connect with people from different backgrounds.

- **Building Bridges, Not Walls:** Instead of building walls of resentment, actively seek understanding and reconciliation, even with those you disagree with.

Remember:

Loving our enemies might seem like a tall order, but it's a call to embrace the transformative power of forgiveness. By letting go of resentment and extending love, we can create a more peaceful and compassionate world.

NOTES:_____
_____
_____
_____
_____
_____
_____
_____
_____
_____
_____
_____
_____
_____
_____
_____
_____
_____
_____
_____

Day 17: Giving to the Needy (Matthew 6:1-4)

Giving Gone Right: It's All About the Motive

Today, Matthew 6:1-4 tackles the act of giving. But Jesus isn't just talking about throwing some coins in a basket. Here, he exposes the pitfall of showy charity and emphasizes the importance of giving with a pure heart.

The Passage: Unveiling the Motive

- (V. 1) Jesus warns against giving for the sake of recognition. True generosity comes from a genuine desire to help, not self-promotion.

- (V. 2) Don't announce your charitable acts. Let your generosity be a quiet act of love, just like God's blessings on us are often unseen.

- (V. 3-4) True giving is done with a pure heart, motivated by compassion and a desire to help others, not by a desire for recognition.

The Lesson: Giving with Authenticity

Charity is a beautiful thing, but the "why" behind it matters. Giving with a pure heart, motivated by love and compassion, brings a deeper reward than any earthly recognition.

Prayer: A Generous Heart

Dear God, help me purify my motives for giving. Grant me the wisdom to give generously with a compassionate heart, seeking to help others without expecting anything in return.

The Challenge: The Generosity Experiment

This week, find a way to give back to your community without seeking recognition. Maybe it's volunteering your time, donating to a cause you care about, or simply offering a helping hand to someone in need.

Interaction

- **Discuss the Impact:** Share stories of times when you've witnessed selfless giving. How did it impact the recipient and the giver?

- **Creative Generosity:** Brainstorm creative ways to be generous in your everyday life. It doesn't have to be grand gestures; small acts of kindness can make a big difference.

Modern Applications: Giving in the Digital Age

Generosity isn't limited to physical acts:

- **Supporting Online Causes:** Many worthy causes have online platforms for donations. Research and support causes you believe in, even with small contributions.

- **Amplifying Good News:** Use social media to share stories of positive change and generosity. Inspire others to get involved and make a difference.

- **Giving Your Time and Skills:** Volunteer your time or skills online. Offer remote consultations, create educational content, or simply lend a listening ear to those who need it.

Remember:

Giving is a powerful tool for making the world a better place. Don't let the desire for recognition overshadow the true beauty of giving – the act of helping others with a genuine and generous heart.

NOTES:

Day 18: Prayer and Authenticity (Matthew 6:5-15)

Prayer Boot Camp: Ditch the Show, Embrace the Real

Today, Matthew 6:5-15 tackles the topic of prayer. Jesus dismantles the idea of showy, public prayers and guides us towards a more authentic and intimate conversation with God.

The Passage: Unveiling the Prayer Game

- (V. 5) Jesus criticizes the practice of public prayer for show. True prayer is a personal conversation with God, not a performance.

- (V. 6) Prayer is a private conversation with God. Find a quiet space where you can connect with Him authentically.

- (V. 7) Avoid long, repetitive prayers. Focus on genuine communication with God, coming from the heart.

- (V. 8) God already knows our needs. Prayer isn't about informing Him, but about expressing our desires, fears, and gratitude.

- (V. 9-13) The Lord's Prayer provides a framework for prayer, but it shouldn't be a rigid script. Use it as a springboard for your own heartfelt conversations with God.

- (V. 14-15) True prayer is intertwined with forgiveness. Holding onto resentment hinders our connection with God.

The Lesson: A Heartfelt Conversation

Prayer isn't about impressing God with eloquence or dramatic performances. It's about cultivating a genuine connection with Him. Come to Him with your joys, sorrows, doubts, and needs. He longs to hear from you, no matter how messy or imperfect your words may be.

Prayer: An Open Heart

Dear God, help me shed the need for pretense in prayer. Grant me the courage to come before you with an open heart, just as I am.

The Challenge: The Authentic Prayer Experiment

This week, commit to spending some quiet time each day in prayer. Focus on having a genuine conversation with God. Express your gratitude, share your burdens, and simply be present with Him.

Interaction

- **Share Your Journey:** Discuss your prayer life with a friend or online community. What are some challenges you face? How can you cultivate a more authentic prayer life?

- **Silence and Reflection:** Research the practice of silent prayer or meditation. Experiment with incorporating quiet reflection into your prayer routine.

Modern Applications: Prayer in a Busy World

Even in our fast-paced lives, we can find moments for prayer:

- **Short & Sweet Prayers:** Throughout your day, offer short prayers of gratitude, for guidance, or simply to connect with God.

- **Prayer Apps & Resources:** Explore prayer apps and online resources that offer guided meditations, prayers for specific situations, or simply inspirational messages.

- **Walking Prayer:** Turn your daily walk into a moving prayer. Reflect on God's presence in nature and offer prayers of thanksgiving.

Remember:

Prayer isn't a performance; it's a lifeline. Come to God authentically, with an open heart, and experience the power of genuine connection with your Creator.

NOTES:_____
_____
_____
_____
_____
_____
_____
_____
_____
_____
_____
_____
_____
_____
_____
_____
_____
_____
_____
_____
_____
_____

Day 19: Treasure in Heaven (Matthew 6:19-24)

Forget Fleeting Riches, Invest in Lasting Treasures

Today's passage, Matthew 6:19-24, tackles the concept of treasure. Jesus challenges our focus on material possessions and urges us to invest in heavenly treasures that hold eternal value.

The Passage: Unveiling True Wealth

- (V. 19-20) Jesus warns against clinging to earthly possessions. They are temporary and can be lost or destroyed. Instead, he encourages us to invest in things that have lasting value – treasures in heaven.

- (V. 21) Our priorities reveal where our hearts truly lie. If we constantly chase after material possessions, our hearts become attached to them.

- (V. 22-23) A healthy eye allows us to see clearly. Focusing on heavenly treasures (true light) brings clarity and purpose to our lives. Focusing solely on earthly possessions (darkness) leads to confusion and a sense of emptiness.

- (V. 24) Serving money and material possessions becomes a form of idolatry. We can't truly serve both God and our desires for earthly riches.

The Lesson: Shifting Our Focus

Jesus isn't advocating for a life of poverty. The point is to avoid letting material possessions control our lives. True wealth lies in our relationship with God, in building a life based on love, service, and spiritual growth. These are the treasures that hold eternal value.

Prayer: Realigning Priorities

Dear God, help me re-evaluate my priorities. Guide me to loosen my grip on material possessions and invest my energy in building a life that reflects your values.

The Challenge: The Treasure Hunt

This week, embark on a "treasure hunt" for things that hold lasting value. Consider:

- Spend time with loved ones.
- Volunteer your time to a cause you care about.

- Learn a new skill or explore your creativity.
- Reflect on your spiritual growth.

Interaction

- **Discuss Your Values:** Share with a friend or online community what truly matters to you in life. What are some ways you can invest in those values?
- **Minimalism Challenge:** Research the concept of minimalism and its impact on happiness. Consider decluttering your physical space to create more mental clarity for focusing on what truly matters.

Modern Applications: Investing in Lasting Riches

In today's consumerist world, it's easy to get caught up in the pursuit of "stuff." Here's how to invest in heavenly treasures:

- **Experiences over Possessions:** Choose experiences that create memories and connections over accumulating more things.
- **Giving Back:** Donating your time, skills, or resources to others is an investment in both their lives and your own spiritual growth.
- **Living Simply:** Focus on living a life of purpose and meaning, not one defined by material possessions.

Remember:

True wealth doesn't come from what we own, but from the richness of our relationships, our connection to something greater than ourselves, and the positive impact we make on the world. Let's invest in treasures that will last an eternity.

NOTES:_____

Day 20: Worry and Trust (Matthew 6:25-34)

Reflection: The Tyranny of "What Ifs?"

We all know the feeling. That gnawing worry in the pit of your stomach, the endless cycle of "what ifs" swirling in your mind. Maybe it's a looming deadline, a difficult relationship, or the general uncertainty of life. Today's passage, Matthew 6:25-34, offers a powerful antidote to worry: trust in God.

The Lesson: Letting Go and Letting God

- (V. 25) Jesus challenges us not to get bogged down by basic needs. He reminds us that life is about more than just material possessions.

- (V. 26) Consider the birds – they don't worry about where their next meal will come from. God provides for them, and He will provide for us as well.

- (V. 27) Worry doesn't change our circumstances; it only steals our joy and peace.

- (V. 28-29) Look at the beauty of the wildflowers – God clothes them in splendor, and He will care for us too.

- (V. 31-33) God knows our needs before we even ask. Our focus should be on seeking Him first, and trusting that He will take care of the rest.

- (V. 33) When we prioritize our relationship with God and live according to His will, He takes care of our needs.

Prayer: Releasing the Burden

Dear God, I confess that worry often weighs me down. Help me to shift my focus from my anxieties to trusting in your love and provision. Give me the strength to let go and allow you to take care of me.

The Challenge: The Worry-Free Zone Experiment

This week, create a "worry-free zone." Set aside a specific time each day to write down your worries. Then, consciously release them to God, offering a prayer of trust. Throughout the day, when worry creeps in, acknowledge it and redirect your thoughts to something positive, like a verse from scripture or a gratitude list.

Interaction

- **Share Your Strategies:** Do you have any practices that help you combat worry? Discuss them with a friend or online community.

- **The Science of Worry:** Research the negative effects of chronic worry on mental and physical health. Share your findings and discuss healthy coping mechanisms.

Modern Applications: Trusting in a Chaotic World

Worry can be especially rampant in our fast-paced, uncertain world:

- **Focus on the Present:** Mindfulness practices like meditation can help you stay grounded in the present moment and reduce anxiety about the future.

- **Practice Gratitude:** Taking time to reflect on the things you're grateful for can shift your perspective and reduce worry.

- **Seek Help:** If worry is overwhelming, don't hesitate to seek professional help from a therapist or counselor.

Remember:

Worry is a thief that steals our joy and peace. By trusting in God's love and provision, we can release our anxieties and experience the freedom that comes from true faith. Let go, and let God take care of you.

NOTES:_____

Weekly Theme Reflection: The Power of Love, Forgiveness, and Trust in God

This week, we've woven together beautiful threads: the transformative power of love, the liberating act of forgiveness, and the unwavering strength of trust in God. As we conclude this exploration, let's reflect on how these elements intertwine, creating a tapestry for a more fulfilling life.

The Everlasting Power of Love

Love, the central theme of countless stories and scriptures, is the cornerstone of a life well-lived. This week, we explored love in its various forms: compassionate love for our fellow beings, forgiving love that heals past hurts, and the unwavering love of God that guides us.

The Challenge: How can we actively cultivate love in our daily lives? Can we extend kindness to those who are difficult, offer forgiveness readily, and express our love to those close to us?

Forgiveness: A Pathway to Freedom

Forgiveness isn't always easy. Holding onto anger and resentment weighs heavily on our hearts. This week, we explored the power of forgiveness, not as a condoning of wrongdoing, but as a liberation from negativity.

The Challenge: Can we identify areas in our lives where forgiveness is needed? Are we willing to release the burdens of anger and resentment, choosing peace and healing instead?

Trusting in the Divine Tapestry

Life can be messy. We face challenges, experience loss, and grapple with uncertainty. This week, we explored the importance of trusting in a higher power, a force greater than ourselves. This trust offers comfort, strength, and guidance amidst life's storms.

The Challenge: How can we cultivate a deeper connection with the divine? Through prayer, meditation, or simply surrendering to a higher purpose, can we strengthen our trust in the grand tapestry of life?

Woven Together: A Life of Meaning

Love, forgiveness, and trust in God are not isolated threads, but rather interconnected strands that create a strong and resilient tapestry.

- **Love allows us to forgive** – When we see others with compassion, we can understand their shortcomings and offer forgiveness.

- **Forgiveness strengthens trust in God** – By letting go of negativity, we open ourselves to the possibility of a higher plan, a plan guided by love.

- **Trust in God empowers love** – Knowing we are supported by a loving force allows us to extend love further, even in difficult circumstances.

Remember:

Weaving these threads into the fabric of our lives is a continuous process. There will be days when love feels challenging, forgiveness seems impossible, and doubt creeps in. But by holding onto these core principles and seeking guidance, we can create a life filled with meaning, connection, and an unwavering sense of purpose.

NOTES:

Week 5: Faith, Miracles, and Following Jesus

Day 21: The Canaanite Woman's Faith (Matthew 15:21-28)

Reflection: Breaking Through Barriers

Today's passage, Matthew 15:21-28, presents the story of the Canaanite woman. This powerful narrative challenges assumptions and highlights the transformative power of persistent faith.

The Lesson: Faith That Breaks Through Walls

- (V. 21-22) The Canaanite woman, an outsider by ethnicity and religion, desperately seeks Jesus' help for her daughter. Initially, Jesus seems unresponsive.

- (V. 23) The disciples, reflecting the prejudices of the time, urge Jesus to dismiss the woman.

- (V. 24) Jesus' initial response seems to confirm her exclusion. But the story takes a surprising turn.

- (V. 25) The woman persists, her faith unwavering. She acknowledges Jesus' authority and pleads for his help.

- (V. 26) Jesus uses a metaphor that reinforces the social and religious barriers between them.

- (V. 27) The woman's response is both clever and insightful. She acknowledges the hierarchy but emphasizes that even scraps of mercy would be enough.

- (V. 28) Jesus recognizes her extraordinary faith and grants her request.

The Challenge: Breaking Down Our Walls

The story challenges us to examine our own prejudices and biases. Do we build walls of exclusion, or are we open to those who seem different?

Prayer: An Open Heart

Dear God, break down any walls of prejudice or judgment that I may have built. Grant me the faith and compassion to see the value in everyone, regardless of background or belief.

Interaction

- **Overcoming Prejudices:** Share your experiences with overcoming personal biases. How can we create a more inclusive and welcoming environment for everyone?

- **The Power of Persistence:** Discuss stories of people who achieved great things through persistence. How can perseverance help us overcome challenges in our own lives?

Modern Applications: Breaking Barriers in Today's World

The story offers valuable lessons for our diverse world:

- **Challenge Stereotypes:** Don't make assumptions about people based on race, religion, or background. Get to know the person behind the label.

- **Embrace Differences:** Diversity is a strength. Seek out opportunities to connect with people from different cultures and walks of life.

- **Advocate for Inclusion:** Speak up against discrimination and prejudice. Create a world where everyone feels welcome and valued.

Remember: Faith can break down walls and bridge divides. The Canaanite woman's story reminds us that God's love and mercy extend to everyone, regardless of background or belief. Let's open our hearts and build bridges of compassion in our world.

NOTES: _____

Day 22: Feeding the Four Thousand (Matthew 15:32-39)

Reflection: Abundance in Unexpected Places

The miracle of the loaves and fishes isn't just a story about Jesus multiplying food. It's a testament to his overflowing compassion and a reminder that God's provision can appear in unexpected places.

The Lesson: Miracles from Scraps

- (V. 32) Jesus' heart goes out to the hungry crowd despite the lack of resources. He is a God who cares for our physical and spiritual well-being.

- (V. 33) The disciples see only the limitations – the vast desert and the meager provisions. They fail to see the boundless power of God.

- (V. 34) Seven loaves and a few fish seem insignificant when faced with a multitude. But in God's hands, even small offerings can become abundant blessings.

- (V. 36) Jesus starts with what they have and offers thanks. Gratitude unlocks the potential for miracles.

- (V. 37) The meager provisions are miraculously multiplied, not just enough to satisfy the hunger, but with leftovers. God's abundance overflows.

Prayer: A Grateful Heart

Dear God, open my eyes to see the potential for miracles in the ordinary. Help me cultivate a heart of gratitude, knowing that you can multiply even the smallest offerings.

The Challenge: The Abundance Experiment

This week, look for opportunities to share what you have, no matter how small. Maybe it's sharing a meal with someone in need, volunteering your time, or simply offering a word of encouragement. Trust that even small acts of generosity can create a ripple effect of abundance.

Interaction

- **The Generosity Chain:** Share stories of times when someone's generosity impacted you. Discuss how acts of giving can create a chain reaction of blessings.

- **Miracles in the Ordinary:** Reflect on everyday miracles you often take for granted: the beauty of nature, the kindness of strangers, or the resilience of the human spirit. Share your reflections with a friend or online community.

Modern Applications: Finding Abundance in a Consumerist World

In a world that often emphasizes "more," the story offers a refreshing perspective:

- **The Sharing Economy:** Explore platforms like community fridges, clothing swaps, or skill-sharing communities that promote resourcefulness and abundance through sharing.

- **Combating Food Waste:** Research the issue of food waste and ways to reduce it at home and in your community.

- **Gratitude Practices:** Cultivate an attitude of gratitude by keeping a gratitude journal or starting a gratitude practice with your family or friends.

Remember:

God's provision is limitless. The miracle of the loaves and fishes reminds us that even in scarcity, there is always something to share. By practicing gratitude and generosity, we can create a world of abundance where everyone has enough.

NOTES:_____

Day 23: The Demand for a Sign (Matthew 16:1-4)

Reflection: Beyond Signs and Spectacles

Today's passage, Matthew 16:1-4, finds the Pharisees and Sadducees tempting Jesus with a request for a sign. This narrative challenges our tendency to prioritize the sensational over the substance.

The Lesson: Discerning the Signs of the Times

- (V. 1) The religious leaders seek a spectacular display of power to validate Jesus' claims. Jesus, however, prioritizes truth and understanding over spectacle.

- (V. 2-3) Jesus criticizes their focus on outward signs while missing the deeper truths unfolding around them. He is the Messiah, the fulfillment of scripture, but they are blinded by their desire for a specific kind of sign.

- (V. 4) Jesus calls out their hypocrisy and lack of faith. The true sign they need is already present - his teachings and his ministry.

Prayer: Eyes to See and Ears to Hear

Dear God, open my eyes to see the signs of your presence in the world around me. Grant me the wisdom to discern truth from spectacle and to focus on the deeper meaning of your message.

The Challenge: Deeper Than Signs

This week, challenge your own need for external validation. Instead of seeking dramatic signs, focus on deepening your understanding of Jesus' teachings. Read a scripture passage each day, reflect on its meaning, and discuss it with a friend or faith leader.

Interaction

- **Faith vs. Spectacle:** Share your thoughts on the role of miracles and signs in faith. How can we ensure our faith is based on more than just sensational experiences?

- **The Signs of Our Times:** Discuss what Jesus might consider the "signs of the times" in our world today. What are the important messages we might be missing if we focus on the sensational?

Modern Applications: Discerning Truth in a Noisy World

In our information age, discernment is crucial:

- **Fact-Checking Information:** Be critical of information you encounter online and in the media. Verify sources and be wary of sensational headlines.

- **Seeking Wisdom over Hype:** Focus on learning from reliable sources and engaging in thoughtful discussions rather than chasing after quick fixes or trendy solutions.

- **The Power of Silence:** Create space for quiet reflection and contemplation in your daily life. This can help you discern truth from noise and connect with your inner wisdom.

Remember: True faith is built on a foundation of understanding and a connection with the divine. While miracles and signs can be awe-inspiring, they shouldn't be the sole basis for our faith. Seek truth, delve deeper into scripture, and allow God to reveal himself to you in the ordinary moments of life.

NOTES:

Day 24: The Cost of Following Jesus (Matthew 16:24-28)

Reflection: The All-In Proposition

Following Jesus isn't a casual commitment. Today's passage, Matthew 16:24-28, lays out the demands of discipleship, urging us to count the cost before embarking on this lifelong journey.

The Lesson: More Than Casual Belief

- **(V. 24-25)** Jesus makes it clear that following him requires sacrifice. We must be willing to put aside our own desires and priorities to embrace his teachings. Taking up the cross symbolizes the willingness to face challenges and even persecution for our faith.

- **(V. 26)** Worldly possessions and achievements pale in comparison to the value of our soul and our relationship with God.

- **(V. 27)** Our choices have consequences. Jesus promises to reward those who remain faithful, even in the face of difficulty.

Prayer: A Committed Heart

Dear God, grant me the courage to count the cost of following you. Help me surrender my own desires and embrace the path you have laid out for me.

The Challenge: The Discipleship Audit

This week, take an honest inventory of your priorities. How much space does your faith truly occupy in your life? Are there areas where you can make adjustments to live a more Christ-centered life?

Interaction

- **Sacrifices for Faith:** Discuss with a friend or online community what sacrifices you've made, or are willing to make, for your faith. How can you support each other on this journey?

- **Living Your Values:** Consider your core values and how they align with your faith. Are there ways you can integrate your values more fully into your daily life?

Modern Applications: Following Jesus in a Secular World

Following Jesus in a world that often prioritizes comfort and self-interest requires intentionality:

- **Living Out Your Faith:** Look for opportunities to share your faith through your actions, not just your words. Volunteer your time, show compassion to others, and live a life that reflects your values.

- **Building a Faith Community:** Find a faith community that supports and challenges you on your spiritual journey. Surround yourself with people who will encourage you to grow in your faith.

- **Facing Challenges with Faith:** Life throws curveballs. Use your faith as a source of strength and guidance when facing difficulties.

Remember: Following Jesus is a lifelong adventure, with both joys and challenges. The cost of discipleship is real, but the rewards are eternal. By counting the cost, making a commitment, and living a life that reflects your faith, you can experience the profound joy and purpose that comes from following Christ.

NOTES:

Day 25: The Transfiguration (Matthew 17:1-8)

Reflection: A Peak Experience

Today's passage, Matthew 17:1-8, recounts the awe-inspiring event of the Transfiguration. Jesus is bathed in light, revealing a glimpse of his divine glory to his closest disciples.

The Lesson: Light in the Darkness

- (V. 1-2) Jesus is transformed on the mountaintop, revealing a radiant light that surpasses anything earthly. This glimpse foreshadows his ultimate victory over death and darkness.

- (V. 3) Moses and Elijah, representing the Law and the Prophets, appear alongside Jesus. This signifies the continuity between Jesus' teachings and the Old Testament.

- (V. 4) Peter, overwhelmed by the experience, suggests making a permanent dwelling on the mountaintop. He doesn't want the experience to end.

- (V. 5-6) A voice from heaven affirms Jesus' identity as the beloved Son of God. The disciples are awestruck and humbled by this divine revelation.

- (V. 7) Jesus, ever compassionate, calms their fear and encourages them not to be afraid.

- (V. 8) The vision fades, but the message remains – Jesus is the Son of God, and his teachings are to be followed.

Prayer: A Yearning for Light

Dear God, grant me a glimpse of your glory, even if it's just a fleeting moment. May your light guide me through the darkness and strengthen my faith in you.

The Challenge: Transformed by the Light

This week, reflect on how you can share the light of Christ with the world. This could be through acts of kindness, words of encouragement, or simply living a life that reflects God's love.

Interaction

- Sharing Spiritual Experiences: Have you ever had a moment of profound spiritual connection? If so, share your experience with a friend or online community.

- **Light in the Dark:** Discuss ways to bring light and hope to those facing difficulties in your community.

Modern Applications: Reflecting God's Light

The story offers inspiration for our own lives:

- **Seeking Spiritual Renewal:** Schedule regular time for prayer, meditation, or reflection to connect with the divine and recharge your spiritual battery.

- **Sharing Your Faith:** Don't be afraid to share your faith with others, both through your words and your actions. Let your light shine brightly!

- **Finding Beauty in the Ordinary:** Look for moments of wonder and beauty in your everyday life. These can be reminders of the divine presence all around us.

Remember:

The Transfiguration offers a glimpse of the divine. While the experience may be temporary, its impact can be lasting. May we carry the light of Christ within us and share it with the world.

NOTES:

Weekly Theme Reflection: Having Faith and Following Jesus' Teachings

This week, we've embarked on a contemplative exploration of faith and its role in following Jesus' teachings. We've encountered stories of unwavering belief, moments of doubt, and ultimately, the transformative power of living according to Jesus' message. As we conclude this theme, let's gather the key takeaways and weave them into the fabric of our lives:

The Seed of Faith: A Personal Journey

Faith, like a seed planted in fertile soil, is a personal journey that unfolds in unique ways for each of us. It can be a deep conviction, a comforting presence, or a guiding light through life's uncertainties.

The Challenge: Reflect on your own faith journey. What has nurtured your faith so far? Are there ways to cultivate a deeper connection with your spiritual core?

Following Jesus: A Path, Not a Destination

Following Jesus' teachings isn't about achieving a perfect state of being, but about embracing a lifelong path of learning and growth. It's about incorporating his principles – love, forgiveness, compassion – into our daily interactions and striving to become better versions of ourselves.

The Challenge: Identify areas in your life where you can better embody Jesus' teachings. How can you demonstrate more love in your relationships, offer forgiveness more readily, or show greater compassion towards others?

Facing Doubt: A Stepping Stone, Not a Stumbling Block

Even the most faithful individuals experience moments of doubt or questioning. This week, we explored how these moments of doubt can be opportunities for introspection and deeper understanding.

The Challenge: When doubt arises, acknowledge it. Can you use this as a chance to re-evaluate your faith or seek guidance from trusted spiritual leaders or communities?

Living with Purpose: The Light We Carry

By having faith and following Jesus' teachings, we discover a sense of purpose. It's about using our gifts and talents to contribute to something larger than ourselves, to make a positive impact on the world around us.

The Challenge: Consider your unique skills and passions. How can you use them to serve others and make a difference in your community or the world?

Remember:

The journey of faith is a lifelong adventure, filled with moments of joy, struggle, and growth. By holding onto your faith, embracing doubt as a natural part of the process, and actively following Jesus' teachings, you can navigate life's path with greater purpose and illuminate the world with the light you carry within.

As we move forward, may the lessons learned this week inspire us to:

- Nurture our individual faith journeys.
- Actively embody Jesus' teachings in our daily lives.
- See doubt as an opportunity for growth and reflection.
- Live with purpose, contributing to the greater good.

May your faith be a guiding force, and may your journey of following Jesus' teachings be filled with joy and fulfillment.

NOTES: _____
_____
_____
_____
_____
_____
_____
_____
_____
_____
_____
_____
_____
_____
_____
_____
_____
_____
_____
_____
_____
_____

Week 6: Confrontation and Controversy

Day 26: Paying the Temple Tax (Matthew 17:24-27)

Reflection: Creative Compliance

Today's passage, Matthew 17:24-27, presents a seemingly simple story about Jesus instructing Peter to pay the temple tax. However, a closer look reveals a nuanced message about fulfilling obligations while staying true to your values.

The Lesson: Beyond Literal Interpretation

- (V. 24) The temple tax was a levy on Jewish men to support the temple in Jerusalem. Jesus and his disciples weren't obligated to pay it, as they were considered Temple personnel.

- "He said, 'Yes.'" (V. 24) Peter, perhaps out of fear of causing trouble, readily agrees that Jesus should pay the tax.

- (V. 25) Jesus, knowing Peter's answer, asks a leading question. He prompts Peter to think critically about the nature of authority and obligation.

- (V. 26) Peter recognizes that a king's children wouldn't be expected to pay taxes to their own father.

- (V. 27) Jesus clarifies that they technically don't have to pay, but to avoid unnecessary conflict, he instructs Peter to miraculously acquire the money to pay the tax.

Prayer: Walking the Tightrope

Dear God, grant me the wisdom to navigate complex situations with integrity and respect for authority. Help me find creative solutions that honor both my beliefs and the needs of others.

The Challenge: The Art of Creative Compliance

This week, consider a situation where you might feel obligated to comply with a rule or expectation that goes against your values. Think creatively about ways to fulfill the basic requirement while staying true to your principles.

Interaction

- **Finding Ethical Solutions:** Share a situation where you had to find a creative solution to an ethical dilemma. How did you approach it?

- **Challenging the Status Quo:** Discuss situations where blindly following the rules can be detrimental. When is it appropriate to challenge the status quo?

Modern Applications: Following Your Moral Compass

The story offers valuable insights for navigating complex situations:

- **Questioning Authority:** Don't blindly accept all rules and regulations. Think critically about their purpose and whether they align with your values.

- **Creative Problem-Solving:** Look for innovative solutions that address the practical need while staying true to your principles.

- **Avoiding Unnecessary Conflict:** Sometimes, strategic compliance can be the best approach to avoid unnecessary disruption.

Remember:

Living a life of integrity means staying true to your values while navigating the complexities of the world. The story of the temple tax reminds us that sometimes, creative solutions are necessary to fulfill obligations while honoring your moral compass.

NOTES:

Day 27: Who is the Greatest? (Matthew 18:1-4)

Reflection: Letting Go of Ego

Today's passage, Matthew 18:1-4, challenges our worldly notions of greatness. Jesus reminds us that true greatness lies in humility and childlike dependence on God.

The Lesson: A Child's Heart

- (V. 1) The disciples, perhaps fueled by ambition or insecurity, ask Jesus about who will have the highest rank in his coming kingdom.

- (V. 2-3) Jesus doesn't answer their question directly. Instead, he uses a child as a symbol of true greatness. Children are innocent, trusting, and free from egotism. These are the qualities we need to cultivate if we want to enter the kingdom of heaven.

Prayer: A Humble Heart

Dear God, help me shed the weight of pride and ambition. Grant me the humility and dependence of a child as I strive to walk in your ways.

The Challenge: Embracing Humility

This week, challenge yourself to be more humble. Actively listen to others, admit your mistakes, and be willing to learn from those around you.

Interaction

- **Redefining Success:** Discuss what true greatness means to you. How does it differ from worldly definitions of success?

- **The Power of Vulnerability:** Share a time when vulnerability and humility led to a positive outcome.

Modern Applications: Humility in a Self-Centered World

The story offers valuable lessons for our self-centered times:

- **Serving Others:** Focus on serving others rather than seeking personal power or recognition. True greatness lies in making a positive impact on the world.

- **Lifelong Learning:** Maintain a childlike curiosity and openness to learning. There's always more to discover and grow from.

- **Leading by Example:** Leaders who are humble and approachable inspire those around them.

Remember:

Greatness in God's eyes is not about status or power. It's about humility, service, and a childlike dependence on Him. Let go of ego and embrace the path of humility on your journey of faith.

NOTES:_____

Day 28: Forgiveness and Reconciliation (Matthew 18:21-35)

Reflection: Letting Go and Letting Love Flow

Today's passage, Matthew 18:21-35, tackles the weighty issue of forgiveness. Jesus emphasizes the importance of forgiving others, not just seven times, but seventy-seven times – a symbolic call for radical and unconditional forgiveness.

The Lesson: Breaking the Cycle of Resentment

- (V. 21) Peter attempts to quantify forgiveness, perhaps reflecting a common practice of the time.

- (V. 22) Jesus shatters Peter's limited perspective. True forgiveness is not a matter of keeping score; it's about releasing resentment and offering unconditional love.

- (V. 23-24) Jesus uses a parable to illustrate the concept of forgiveness. The king represents God, and the servant represents us, with our debts of sin.

- (V. 25-27) The servant pleads for forgiveness, and the king, filled with compassion, cancels the debt.

- (V. 28-30) However, the forgiven servant shows no mercy to his fellow servant who owes him a much smaller debt. He throws him in prison, demonstrating the hypocrisy of those who refuse to forgive others after being forgiven themselves.

- (V. 31-34) The king, learning of the unforgiving servant's actions, is enraged. He takes back his forgiveness and punishes the servant harshly.

- (V. 35) Jesus concludes by emphasizing the consequences of unforgiveness. Just as God forgives us, we are called to forgive others.

Prayer: A Heart of Forgiveness

Dear God, grant me the strength to forgive those who have wronged me. Help me release resentment and cultivate a heart of compassion and love.

The Challenge: The Forgiveness Experiment

This week, choose to forgive someone who has hurt you. This doesn't mean forgetting what happened, but rather letting go of the negativity associated with it. Consider writing a letter to the person (that you may or may not send) expressing your forgiveness.

Interaction

- **The Burden of Unforgiveness:** Discuss the emotional and spiritual toll of holding onto unforgiveness. How can we begin to let go?

- **Seeking Forgiveness:** Have you ever had to ask someone for forgiveness? Share your experience (without revealing identifying details).

Modern Applications: Building Bridges in a Divided World

Forgiveness is essential for healing relationships and fostering peace:

- **Practicing Compassion:** Actively cultivate compassion for others, even those who have wronged you. Understanding their motivations can help you forgive.

- **Breaking the Cycle of Hurt:** Choosing forgiveness disrupts the cycle of resentment and retaliation that can perpetuate conflict. By forgiving others, we create opportunities for reconciliation and healing.

- **Promoting Reconciliation:** Forgiveness doesn't always lead to restored relationships, but it opens the door to the possibility. When appropriate, seek reconciliation with those you've forgiven.

Remember:

Forgiveness is an ongoing journey, not a one-time event. It takes time and effort, but the rewards are immense. By releasing resentment and offering forgiveness, we experience greater peace, open ourselves to deeper connections, and live in accordance with the teachings of Jesus.

Day 29: Divorce and Remarriage (Matthew 19:3-12)

Reflection: Beyond Right and Wrong

Today's passage, Matthew 19:3-12, tackles the sensitive topic of divorce and remarriage. Jesus' words have been debated for centuries, reflecting the complexity of human relationships. This session moves beyond a simple right-or-wrong approach, inviting us to consider the deeper meaning behind the text.

The Lesson: The Weight of Commitment

- (V. 3) The Pharisees pose a question designed to trap Jesus. Divorce was a common practice, but there were differing interpretations of Mosaic Law on acceptable grounds.

- (V. 4) Jesus starts by reminding them of marriage's foundation – the divinely ordained union of a man and woman.

- (V. 5) He emphasizes the sacred nature of marriage, a lifelong commitment between two people.

- (V. 6) Jesus affirms the permanence of marriage, ideally intended to last a lifetime. However, the following verse acknowledges the complexity of human relationships.

- (V. 7) The Pharisees point to a provision in Deuteronomy allowing divorce.

- (V. 8) Jesus clarifies that Moses' concession to divorce was a concession to the Israelites' stubbornness, not God's original intention.

- (V. 9) Jesus offers a stricter interpretation, allowing divorce only in cases of marital infidelity. This teaching has been debated throughout Christian history.

Prayer: For Compassion and Understanding

Dear God, grant me wisdom and compassion when navigating the complexities of relationships. Help me understand the weight of commitment and the importance of upholding sacred vows.

The Challenge: Honoring Vows and Facing Reality

This week, reflect on the importance of honoring vows made in marriage.

However, acknowledge that some situations may necessitate difficult choices.

Interaction

- **The Impact of Divorce:** Share (without disclosing private details) how divorce has impacted your life or the lives of someone you know.

- **Beyond Legalism:** Discuss the limitations of a strictly legalistic approach to divorce. What other factors need to be considered when facing such a decision?

- **Seeking Support:** Explore the importance of seeking support from trusted friends, family, or religious leaders when navigating the challenges of divorce.

Modern Applications: Marriage in a Changing World

The passage offers timeless insights for navigating marriage in a complex world:

- **Strengthening Communication:** Invest in open and honest communication with your spouse. Learn to listen deeply and express your needs effectively.

- **Prioritizing Commitment:** Remember the vows you took and the importance of working through challenges together.

- **Seeking Help When Needed:** There's no shame in seeking professional help from a marriage counselor or therapist if you're facing difficulties.

Remember:

Marriage is a complex journey, and navigating divorce can be even more challenging. Jesus' message emphasizes the importance of honoring vows, but also acknowledges the realities of human relationships. Approach these situations with compassion, understanding, and a willingness to seek guidance when needed.

Day 30: Letting the Little Children Come (Matthew 19:13-15)

Reflection: Open Hearts, Open Doors

Today's passage, Matthew 19:13-15, offers a heartwarming scene of Jesus interacting with children. This simple story holds profound lessons about humility, openness, and the importance of welcoming all into God's embrace.

The Lesson: Embracing Childlike Wonder

- (V. 13) People bring their children to Jesus for a blessing, but the disciples try to shoo them away. Perhaps they see the children as unimportant or a nuisance.

- (V. 14) Jesus rebukes the disciples and welcomes the children. He recognizes that the kingdom of heaven belongs to those with a childlike spirit – innocent, trusting, and open to God's love.

- (V. 15) Jesus blesses the children, acknowledging their place in God's kingdom.

Prayer: A Childlike Heart

Dear God, help me shed the weight of cynicism and pride. Grant me the openness and wonder of a child as I approach you and navigate the world.

The Challenge: Embracing All Who Seek God

This week, challenge yourself to be more welcoming and inclusive. Open your heart to those who may seem different or excluded.

Interaction

- **The Power of Innocence:** Discuss the positive qualities associated with children – their trust, openness, and sense of wonder. How can we cultivate these qualities in ourselves?

- **Who Feels Unwelcome?:** Consider people who might feel excluded from your church or community. How can you create a more welcoming space?

Modern Applications: Openness in a Divided World

The story offers valuable insights for fostering a more inclusive world:

- **Breaking Down Barriers:** Challenge biases and prejudices that create divisions. Seek common ground and celebrate diversity.

- **Mentoring the Young:** Invest time and energy in mentoring children and youth. Nurture their innocence and sense of wonder.

- **Welcoming All Seekers:** Our communities of faith should be open to anyone seeking a connection with God, regardless of background or experience.

Remember:

Jesus' message is clear – the kingdom of heaven belongs to those with open hearts and a childlike spirit. Let us strive for humility, inclusivity, and a genuine welcome for all who seek God's love.

NOTES:

Weekly Theme Reflection: Facing Challenges and Standing by Jesus' Teachings

NOTES:_____

Week 7: Teaching on Discipleship and the Kingdom

Day 31: The Rich Young Ruler (Matthew 19:16-30)

Reflection: True Wealth

Today's passage, Matthew 19:16-30, tells the story of the rich young ruler. This encounter challenges our understanding of wealth and true fulfillment in life.

The Lesson: More Than Possessions

- (V. 16) A rich young ruler approaches Jesus, seeking the key to eternal life. He seems to believe good deeds are the answer.

- (V. 17) Jesus redirects the question, emphasizing that true goodness comes from God. He also reminds the ruler of the importance of following God's commandments.

- (V. 20) The young ruler assures Jesus he has followed the commandments faithfully. He's perplexed – what more is needed?

- (V. 21) Jesus challenges him to take a radical step – letting go of his wealth and following him. True treasure lies in a relationship with God, not material possessions.

- (V. 22) The young ruler is unwilling to give up his wealth. He walks away disappointed, highlighting the difficulty of letting go of worldly attachments.

Prayer: A Heart Set on God

Dear God, help me discern what truly matters in life. May I not be consumed by material possessions but focus on building a relationship with you and living according to your will.

The Challenge: Letting Go of What Holds Us Back

This week, reflect on what possessions or attachments might be hindering your spiritual growth. Consider simplifying your life and focusing on the things that truly matter.

Interaction

- **Defining Wealth:** Discuss what true wealth means to you. Does it go beyond material possessions?

- **The Challenge of Letting Go:** Share a time when you had to let go of something important to you. What did you learn from the experience?

Modern Applications: Finding Fulfillment in a Materialistic World

The story offers valuable insights for navigating our materialistic world:

- **Living Simply:** Consider practicing minimalism or adopting a more sustainable lifestyle. Focus on experiences and relationships rather than accumulating possessions.

- **Generosity:** Cultivate a spirit of generosity. Share your time, resources, and talents with those in need.

- **Finding Purpose Beyond Work:** Don't define your worth by your career or possessions. Seek a deeper purpose in life that aligns with your values and brings you fulfillment.

Remember:

Jesus doesn't condemn wealth itself, but the attachment to it. True happiness and fulfillment come from following God's will and letting go of what hinders our spiritual growth. Let this be a reminder to examine your priorities and seek the treasures that truly last.

NOTES:

Day 32: The Laborers in the Vineyard (Matthew 20:1-16)

Reflection: Beyond What We Earn

Today's passage, Matthew 20:1-16, presents the parable of the laborers in the vineyard. This story challenges our conventional understanding of fairness and rewards, highlighting the unexpected generosity of God's grace.

The Lesson: God's Generous Grace

- (V. 1) The parable begins with a landowner hiring workers for his vineyard at different times of the day.

- (V. 2) The first group agrees to work for the standard wage of a denarius for a day's labor.

- (V. 3-4) The landowner hires more workers throughout the day, not guaranteeing a specific wage but promising fair compensation.

- (V. 4) These workers trust the landowner and agree to his terms.

- (V. 5) The landowner continues to hire workers throughout the day.

- (V. 6) Even near the end of the workday, the landowner finds some unemployed men and offers them work.

- (V. 7) These workers haven't worked all day, but the landowner gives them the same opportunity.

- (V. 8) At the end of the day, the landowner instructs his foreman to pay the workers, starting with the last hired group.

- (V. 9) Surprisingly, the last-minute workers receive the full daily wage, just like those who had toiled all day.

- (V. 10) The first group, expecting a higher payout for their longer hours, grumble when they receive the same amount.

- (V. 11-12) They feel cheated, believing they deserve more due to their longer hours.

- (V. 13-14) The landowner reminds them of the agreed-upon wage and his right to be generous with his own resources.

- (V. 15) He challenges their envy and emphasizes his freedom to be gracious.

- (V. 16) Jesus concludes by emphasizing that God's grace can overturn our human expectations of fairness.

Prayer: A Heart of Gratitude

Dear God, open my eyes to the abundance of your grace. Help me appreciate your generosity and move beyond a limited understanding of fairness.

The Challenge: Practicing Generosity

This week, challenge yourself to be more generous with your time, resources, and forgiveness. Focus on acts of kindness that go beyond what is expected.

Interaction

- **Fairness vs. Grace:** Discuss the concept of fairness and how it compares to God's grace. Can they coexist?

- **Earning vs. Receiving:** Explore the difference between earning something through work and receiving it as a gift. How does this parable challenge our ideas about merit and reward?

Modern Applications: Grace in Everyday Life

The parable offers valuable insights for living in a world obsessed with achievement:

- **Focus on the Gift:** Recognize the blessings in your life, not just the things you've earned through hard work.

- **Practice Random Acts of Kindness:** Look for opportunities to show unexpected generosity to others, big or small.

- **Letting Go of Resentment:** Release yourself from the burden of envy and resentment. Celebrate the good fortune of others.

Remember:

The parable reminds us that God's grace operates on a different level than human fairness. We are all recipients of undeserved blessings. Let this story inspire you to practice generosity, appreciate God's grace, and move beyond a self-centered perspective.

Day 33: Blind Bartimaeus Healed (Matthew 20:29)

Reflection: Beyond Physical Sight

Today's passage, Matthew 20:29-34, tells the story of Blind Bartimaeus. This heartwarming narrative reminds us that Jesus has the power to heal not only physical blindness but also the blindness of the heart and mind.

The Lesson: Seeing What Matters Most

- (V. 29) Bartimaeus, a blind man, sits by the road as Jesus and his followers pass through Jericho.

- (V. 30) Bartimaeus recognizes Jesus and calls out for mercy, acknowledging his power to heal.

- (V. 31) Despite attempts to silence him, Bartimaeus persists in his plea for healing.

- (V. 32) Jesus hears Bartimaeus' cries and instructs the crowd to bring him closer.

- (V. 32) Bartimaeus throws off his cloak, demonstrating his eagerness and faith in Jesus.

- (V. 33) Jesus asks Bartimaeus what he desires, and the man expresses his longing to see again.

- (V. 34) Jesus grants Bartimaeus his request, highlighting the power of his faith. Bartimaeus is healed and follows Jesus.

Prayer: For Open Eyes and Hearts

Dear God, open my eyes to see the world around me with clarity and compassion. Help me see beyond the surface and recognize the needs of others.

The Challenge: Seeking Spiritual Sight

This week, reflect on areas in your life where you might be experiencing a form of blindness. Seek guidance from God to see things more clearly.

Interaction

- **Blind Spots:** Discuss areas in our lives where we might be spiritually blind – prejudice, biases, or neglecting those in need.

- **The Power of Faith:** Share stories of how faith has helped you overcome challenges or find hope in difficult times.

Modern Applications: Seeing Beyond the Obvious

The story offers valuable insights for navigating the complexities of life:

- **Seeking Inner Healing:** Recognize that healing goes beyond the physical. Seek spiritual guidance and support for emotional and mental well-being.

- **Compassion for the Marginalized:** Pay attention to those who are often overlooked or unheard. Advocate for those who are struggling.

- **The Importance of Persistence:** Don't be afraid to raise your voice and ask for help when you need it.

Remember:

The story of Blind Bartimaeus reminds us that Jesus has the power to heal our physical and spiritual blindness. By seeking his guidance and cultivating faith, we can learn to see the world with greater clarity, compassion, and purpose.

NOTES:

Day 34: The Parable of the Unexpected Feast (Luke 14:15-24)

Reflection: Who is Invited to the Table?

Today's scripture, Luke 14:15-24, presents the Parable of the Unexpected Feast. This story challenges us to re-evaluate who we consider worthy of our time and hospitality.

An Invitation Extended

- (V. 15) A dinner guest expresses his longing to participate in the future Messianic banquet.

- (V. 16) Jesus responds with a parable, introducing a host who invites a large group of people.

- (V. 17) The host sends out a servant to inform the guests that the feast is prepared, signaling the time to arrive.

Excuses and Rejections

- "But they all alike began to make excuses. The first said to him, 'I have bought a field, and I must go out and see it. Please have me excused.'" (V. 18)

- "Another said, 'I have bought five yoke of oxen, and I am going to test them. Please have me excused.'" (V. 19)

- (V. 20) One by one, the invited guests offer flimsy excuses to avoid the feast.

A Change of Course

- (V. 21) The host, disappointed by the rejections, instructs his servant to invite those who were initially overlooked.

- (V. 22) The servant completes his task, but there's still space remaining at the table.

- (V. 23) The host, determined to fill the table, instructs the servant to invite anyone they encounter, regardless of social status.

- (V. 24) Jesus concludes the parable, highlighting the unexpected turn of events. Those who initially declined are excluded, while others now have the opportunity to experience the host's generosity.

Prayer: Open Hearts and Inclusive Love

Dear God, help us cultivate open hearts and a spirit of inclusion. May we extend your love and hospitality to all, regardless of background or status.

The Challenge: Rethinking Hospitality

This week, consider how you approach hospitality in your daily life. Are there ways you can be more inclusive and welcoming to others?

Interaction

- **The Importance of Hospitality:** Discuss the concept of hospitality and its role in building relationships and strengthening communities.

- **Redefining "The Least of These":** Explore the concept of welcoming those who are often excluded or marginalized. How can we ensure everyone feels welcome at our tables (physical or metaphorical)?

Modern Applications: Building Bridges

The Parable of the Unexpected Feast offers valuable insights for creating a more inclusive world:

- **Looking Beyond Appearances:** The story reminds us to look beyond outward appearances and extend kindness to all.

- **The Power of Community:** Building strong communities requires hospitality and a willingness to welcome others.

- **Unexpected Blessings:** Sometimes, opening our hearts and extending hospitality can lead to unexpected blessings and connections.

Remember:

The Parable of the Unexpected Feast challenges us to re-evaluate our societal norms and redefine who is worthy of our love and attention. Let this story inspire you to create a more welcoming and inclusive environment in your own life.

Day 35: Cleansing the Temple (Matthew 21:12-17)

Today's passage, Matthew 21:12-17, recounts Jesus' dramatic act of cleansing the temple. This event challenges us to consider the true purpose of sacred spaces and the importance of authentic worship.

The Lesson: Honoring the Sacred

- (V. 12) Jesus enters the temple and disrupts the commercial activity taking place. Money changers and merchants were using the temple for personal gain.

- (V. 13) Jesus quotes scripture, emphasizing that the temple is intended for prayer and communion with God, not commercial activity. He condemns their actions as robbery.

- (V. 14) Following the cleansing, Jesus focuses on his true purpose – healing the sick and offering spiritual guidance.

- (V. 15) The religious leaders are upset by Jesus' actions and the growing support he receives from the crowds.

- (V. 16) Jesus defends his actions and uses scripture to highlight that even children recognize God's work.

Prayer: For a Renewed Heart

Dear God, help me approach sacred spaces with reverence and a desire for genuine worship. May my heart be a temple dedicated to you, free from distractions and focused on your presence.

The Challenge: Creating Sacred Space

This week, consider how you can create sacred space in your daily life. This could involve setting aside time for prayer and reflection, finding a quiet place for meditation, or simply approaching your surroundings with a sense of awe.

Interaction

- **The Purpose of Sacred Spaces:** Discuss the role of temples, churches, mosques, or other sacred spaces in your life. What purpose do they serve?

- **Distractions in Worship:** Explore the various distractions that can hinder genuine worship. How can we create a more focused and meaningful experience?

Modern Applications: Reclaiming the Sacred

The story offers valuable insights for a world often focused on the material:

- **Prioritizing Spiritual Growth:** Make time for spiritual practices like prayer, meditation, or spending time in nature.

- **Challenging Injustice:** Speak out against commercialism and exploitation that might be present in religious institutions.

- **Authentic Worship:** Focus on the essence of worship – connecting with God, seeking guidance, and offering gratitude.

Remember:

The cleansing of the temple reminds us that sacred spaces are for encountering the divine, not personal gain or distractions. Let this story inspire you to create sacred space in your life and prioritize authentic worship in your relationship with God.

NOTES:

Day 36: Parables of Warning (Matthew 21-22)

Today's passage, Matthew 21:28-22:14, features a series of parables spoken by Jesus. These parables serve as warnings, urging listeners to be faithful stewards and prepare for God's judgment.

The Lesson: Living a Fruitful Life

- (V. 28) The first parable (The Two Sons) tells the story of a father who asks his sons to work in his vineyard.

- (V. 29) The first son initially refuses but later obeys his father.

- (V. 30) The second son promises to go but ultimately disobeys.

- (V. 31-32) Jesus emphasizes that actions speak louder than words. Even those considered outsiders can be forgiven if they repent and follow God.

- (V. 32) Jesus criticizes the religious leaders for rejecting John the Baptist's message of repentance, while those on the margins embraced it.

- (V. 33) The second parable (The Wicked Tenants) compares God's kingdom to a vineyard entrusted to unfaithful tenants.

- (V. 34) The landowner sends servants to collect his share of the harvest.

- (V. 35) The tenants mistreat and even kill the landowner's servants.

- (V. 36) The landowner sends more servants, hoping for a better outcome, but they suffer the same fate.

- (V. 37) In desperation, the landowner sends his own son, believing they will show him respect.

- (V. 38) The tenants plot to kill the son and seize the inheritance.

- (V. 38) They carry out their evil plan, murdering the son.

- (V. 39-40) Jesus warns that the landowner will punish the wicked tenants and entrust the vineyard to new caretakers.

Prayer: For Open Hearts and Obedience

Dear God, grant me a heart that is receptive to your will. Help me live a life that bears good fruit and honors your purpose.

The Challenge: Living a Responsible Life

This week, reflect on your role as a steward of God's resources – your time, talents, and possessions. How can you use them wisely and productively?

Interaction

- **The Parable's Message:** Discuss the central themes of the parables – obedience, repentance, and judgment.

- **Living a Fruitful Life:** Explore what it means to live a life that bears good fruit. How can we cultivate a life of purpose and service?

Modern Applications: Taking Responsibility

The parables offer valuable insights for living responsibly in today's world:

- **Fulfilling Our Commitments:** Be a person of your word. Follow through on commitments you make to God, family, friends, and employers.

- **Wise Stewardship:** Recognize that we are all stewards of something – time, resources, talents. Use them wisely and responsibly for the benefit of others.

- **Repentance and Change:** It's never too late to course-correct. Acknowledge past mistakes and actively seek forgiveness and change.

- **Recognizing God's Ownership:** Remember that ultimately, everything belongs to God. We are called to be faithful caretakers, not self-serving owners.

Remember:

These parables serve as a wake-up call. They urge us to be responsible stewards, live with purpose, and prepare ourselves for God's ultimate judgment. By embracing a life of obedience, repentance, and service, we can bear good fruit and contribute positively to the world around us.

Holy Week:

Day 37: Palm Sunday: The Triumphant Entry (Matthew 21:1-11)

Reflection: The Unexpected King

Today's passage, Matthew 21:1-11, recounts Jesus' triumphant entry into Jerusalem. This event challenges our expectations of power and leadership, reminding us that God often works in unexpected ways.

A King Unlike Any Other

- (V. 1) Jesus arrives near Jerusalem, a city synonymous with power and authority.

- (V. 2) Jesus instructs his disciples to find a donkey and her colt, a humble mode of transportation.

- (V. 3) The act of requisitioning the animals highlights Jesus' authority, yet the choice of a donkey subverts expectations of a conquering king.

- (V. 4-5) Jesus' actions fulfill a prophecy, portraying him as a gentle and humble king, not a powerful warrior.

- (V. 6) The disciples obey, demonstrating trust and following Jesus' unconventional lead.

- (V. 7) Jesus mounts the colt, a symbol of peace, not a warhorse.

- (V. 8) The crowds celebrate Jesus' arrival, recognizing him as their king despite his humble appearance.

- (V. 9) The people declare Jesus king, praising and welcoming him.

- (V. 10) The city is in a frenzy, but many are confused by Jesus' unassuming presence.

Prayer: Openness to God's Work

Dear God, help me shed my preconceived notions about what following you looks like. Grant me the humility and openness to recognize your presence and purpose, even in unexpected forms.

The Challenge: Following an Unconventional Leader

This week, consider the ways Jesus challenges traditional notions of leadership. How can we embrace a more humble and service-oriented approach in our own lives?

Interaction

- **Redefining Power:** Discuss the concept of power and leadership. How does Jesus' entry into Jerusalem challenge our understanding?

- **Following Jesus:** Explore the challenges and rewards of following Jesus, even when it means embracing the unexpected.

Modern Applications: Seeking Truth Beyond Appearances

The story offers valuable insights for a world obsessed with outward appearances:

- **Looking Beyond the Surface:** Don't judge people or situations based solely on first impressions. Seek truth and value beyond the superficial.

- **The Power of Humility:** True leadership is often rooted in humility and service, not outward displays of power.

- **Openness to God's Work:** Be open to God's work in your life, even when it takes unexpected forms.

Remember:

The Palm Sunday story reminds us that Jesus's kingdom operates differently than earthly kingdoms. He is a king who comes in humility, seeking service, not domination. Let this story challenge your expectations and inspire you to follow Jesus on his unconventional path.

NOTES:_____
_____
_____
_____
_____
_____
_____
_____
_____
_____
_____
_____
_____
_____
_____
_____
_____
_____
_____
_____
_____
_____
_____

Day 38: Monday: The Great Commission (Matthew 28:16-20)

Reflection: Sharing the Good News

Today's passage, Matthew 28:16-20, recounts Jesus' final words to his disciples after his resurrection. This passage, known as the Great Commission, equips and empowers believers to spread the message of Christianity throughout the world.

The Mission Entrusted

- (V. 16) The disciples, forever changed by Jesus' life, death, and resurrection, gather at a designated mountain.

- (V. 17) The disciples encounter the risen Jesus, filled with a mix of awe and doubt.

- (V. 18) Jesus reassures them of his power and authority, emphasizing his divine nature.

- (V. 19) Jesus entrusts his disciples with a critical mission – to make disciples of all nations. This marks the beginning of the spread of Christianity.

- (V. 20) Jesus equips them with the task of teaching new believers and offers a comforting promise of his constant presence.

Prayer: A Willing Heart for Service

Dear God, ignite a passion in my heart to share your message with others. Grant me the courage and wisdom to faithfully fulfill your commission.

The Challenge: Spreading the Gospel

This week, reflect on how you can share your faith with others. It doesn't have to be grand gestures; even small acts of kindness and compassion can be powerful testimonies.

Interaction

- **The Great Commission Today:** Discuss the meaning and relevance of the Great Commission in the modern world. How can we share our faith effectively in our current context?

- **Sharing Your Story:** Explore different ways to share your faith journey with others. Consider opportunities for personal conversations, acts of service, or participation in outreach programs.

Modern Applications: Living the Message

The Great Commission offers valuable insights for living a life of faith:

- **Sharing Your Faith:** Seek opportunities to share your faith journey with others through words and actions.

- **Living as an Example:** Live a life that reflects the teachings of Jesus, demonstrating love, compassion, and service.

- **The Ongoing Mission:** The spread of Christianity is an ongoing mission. We are all called to play a role in sharing the message of hope and salvation.

Remember:

The Great Commission reminds us that Jesus' message is not meant to be contained. We are all called to be active participants in sharing the good news of God's love and grace with the world.

NOTES:

Day 39: Whose Image? Taxes and Authority (Matthew 22:15-22)

Reflection: Render Unto Caesar

Today's passage, Matthew 22:15-22, presents a challenging exchange between Jesus and the religious leaders. They attempt to trap him with a question about paying taxes to the Roman authorities.

A Test of Loyalty

- (V. 15) The Pharisees, a powerful religious group, deliberately try to trick Jesus with a loaded question.

- (V. 16-17) The Pharisees and Herodians (supporters of Roman rule) approach Jesus with a seemingly innocent question. However, their motive is to create a conflict – if Jesus says "yes," he appears to condone Roman rule. If he says "no," he can be accused of rebellion.

- (V. 18) Jesus sees through their ploy and exposes their hypocrisy.

- (V. 19) Jesus asks for the coin used to pay the tax, initiating a fascinating object lesson.

- (V. 20) Jesus points out the image of Caesar on the coin, highlighting the Roman authority behind the currency.

- (V. 21) Jesus delivers his famous response, urging a distinction between earthly and heavenly authority. We should fulfill our obligations to the government while also prioritizing our devotion to God.

- (V. 22) The religious leaders are left speechless by Jesus' wisdom and his ability to navigate a complex question.

Prayer: For Discernment and Faithfulness

Dear God, grant me wisdom to navigate the complexities of life. Help me to discern your will and fulfill my obligations with integrity and faith.

The Challenge: Balancing Loyalties

This week, consider the situations in your life where multiple loyalties might come into play. How can you navigate these situations with honesty and integrity?

Interaction

- **Render to Caesar:** Discuss the meaning of Jesus' statement and its application in today's world. What are our obligations to both secular and religious authorities?

- **Faith and Social Responsibility:** Explore how faith can guide our involvement in society and our understanding of our roles as citizens.

Modern Applications: Balancing Authority and Faith

The passage offers valuable insights for living in a world with competing demands:

- **Discerning Right from Wrong:** Faith can guide us in making ethical decisions, even when faced with pressure to conform.

- **Balancing Loyalties:** We can be responsible citizens while remaining true to our core values and beliefs.

- **Living with Integrity:** Seek to live authentically, fulfilling obligations with honesty and without compromising your faith.

Remember:

The story of the tax question reminds us that navigating authority is a complex issue. Jesus' response emphasizes the importance of discernment and living with integrity, honoring both earthly and divine obligations.

NOTES:

Day 40: The Weight of Choice: Judas' Betrayal (Matthew 26:14-16)

Reflection: A Fork in the Road

Today's passage, Matthew 26:14-16, marks a pivotal moment in Jesus' ministry – Judas' betrayal. This act of treachery challenges us to consider the weight of our choices and the power of redemption.

The Seeds of Betrayal

- (V. 14) The narrative introduces Judas, one of Jesus' twelve disciples, making a fateful decision.

- (V. 14) Judas' motivation is revealed – he seeks personal gain in exchange for betraying Jesus.

- (V. 15) The chief priests agree to Judas' price, solidifying the act of betrayal.

- (V. 16) Judas actively searches for ways to deliver Jesus into their hands, setting in motion a chain of events leading to Jesus' crucifixion.

Prayer: For Strength and Forgiveness

Dear God, help me to make choices that align with your will. Grant me the strength to resist temptation and the courage to seek forgiveness when I fall short.

The Challenge: The Power of Choice

This week, consider the power of your choices and their impact on yourself and others. How can you make choices that lead to positive outcomes?

Interaction

- **The Weight of Decisions:** Discuss the significance of our choices and the potential consequences.

- **Redemption and Forgiveness:** Explore the concept of redemption. Is it always possible to find forgiveness, even after making a grave mistake?

Modern Applications: Choosing Integrity

The story offers valuable lessons for navigating complex situations:

- **Temptation and Choice:** We all face temptation. The key is to recognize it and choose the right path.

- **The Power of Forgiveness:** Even in the face of betrayal, forgiveness can offer a path toward healing and renewal.

- **The Importance of Integrity:** Living with integrity requires making choices that align with your values, even when it's difficult.

Remember:

Judas' betrayal reminds us of the human capacity for both good and evil. It is a stark reminder of the importance of our choices and the power of seeking forgiveness. This story also introduces the events leading to Jesus' sacrifice, a theme explored further in the coming days of Holy Week.

NOTES: _____

Thursday: The Last Supper (Matthew 26:17-30)

Reflection: A Lesson in Humility

Today's passage, John 13:3-17, recounts Jesus' powerful act of washing his disciples' feet on the eve of his crucifixion. This act serves as a profound lesson in humility and service.

A Reversal of Roles

- (V. 3) The passage establishes Jesus' divine nature and his awareness of his upcoming sacrifice.

- (V. 4) Jesus sets aside his garments, signifying a servant's posture.

- (V. 5) Jesus takes on the role of a servant, performing a task typically done by the lowest in social hierarchy.

- (V. 6) Peter is surprised and initially resists, reflecting societal norms.

- (V. 7) Jesus assures Peter that the meaning will become clear in time.

- (V. 8) Jesus emphasizes the importance of this act, linking it to spiritual connection.

- (V. 9) Peter, after understanding the significance, fully submits to Jesus' action.

- (V. 10) Jesus clarifies that some (Judas) are not fully committed.

- (V. 11) Jesus foreshadows Judas' betrayal, highlighting the contrast between humility and betrayal.

- (V. 12) Jesus reiterates the importance of the act.

- (V. 13-14) Jesus commands his disciples to follow his example of humility and service.

- (V. 15) Jesus emphasizes that this act is not a one-time event, but a model for their behavior.

Prayer: For a Servant's Heart

Dear God, cultivate a spirit of humility and service within me. Help me prioritize the needs of others and approach life with a servant's heart.

The Challenge: Living with Humility

This week, reflect on the ways you can embody humility in your daily interactions. Seek opportunities to serve others, even in small ways.

Interaction

- **The Power of Humility:** Discuss the concept of humility and its importance in our relationships with God and others.

- **Servant Leadership:** Explore the idea of leadership through service. How can we lead by example and prioritize the well-being of those we lead?

Modern Applications: Serving Others

The story offers valuable insights for building strong relationships and fostering a more compassionate world:

- **Leading by Example:** True leaders prioritize service and humility over self-importance.

- **Serving Others:** Seek opportunities to serve others, even in small ways. These acts can have a significant impact.

- **Humility in Relationships:** Humility is essential for building strong and lasting relationships.

Remember: The washing of the feet is a powerful reminder that true greatness lies in serving others. Jesus, the ultimate leader, demonstrates this principle through his actions. Let this story inspire you to approach life with humility and prioritize the needs of those around you

NOTES:_____

Good Friday: The Crucifixion (Matthew 27:32-66)

That's right! Today is Good Friday, a day commemorating the crucifixion of Jesus Christ. Here's a look at the passage you requested, Matthew 27:32-66, focusing on the profound sacrifice and its impact:

Reflection: A Sacrifice of Love

Today's passage, Matthew 27:32-66, recounts the harrowing events of Jesus' crucifixion. This act of self-sacrifice lies at the heart of the Christian faith, representing God's immense love for humanity.

The Path to Calvary

- (V. 32) Jesus, weakened and burdened by the weight of the cross, is forced to endure this additional suffering.

- (V. 33) The place of execution is a grim reminder of the brutality associated with crucifixion.

- (V. 34) Jesus is offered a drink to numb the pain, but he refuses, choosing to face his suffering fully.

- (V. 35) The soldiers fulfill a prophecy about dividing Jesus' clothes, adding another layer of symbolic meaning.

- (V. 36) The soldiers tasked with guarding Jesus embody the forces of human cruelty.

- (V. 37) The inscription on the cross mocks Jesus' claim of kingship, yet it also proclaims his true identity to the world.

The Moment of Sacrifice

- (V. 39-40) The crowd taunts Jesus, questioning his power and divinity.

- (V. 41-42) Even the religious leaders add to the mockery, further intensifying the pain.

- (V. 43) Despite the suffering and humiliation, Jesus remains faithful to God.

- (V. 44) Even the criminals condemned alongside Jesus join in the taunts, highlighting the depth of human cruelty.

Darkness and Light

- (V. 45) An unnatural darkness descends, symbolizing the gravity of the moment and the withdrawal of God's presence.

- (V. 46) Facing the full weight of sin and separation from God, Jesus cries out in anguish.

- (V. 47) Even in Jesus' moment of despair, there's a misunderstanding, highlighting the confusion surrounding the event.

- (V. 48) An act of (misguided) mercy is offered, reflecting a flicker of humanity amidst the brutality.

- (V. 49) Some remain skeptical, highlighting the lack of faith present.

- (V. 50) Jesus lets out a final cry and surrenders his spirit, marking the culmination of his sacrifice.

- (V. 51) These dramatic events signify the profound impact of Jesus' death, shaking the very foundations of the religious establishment.

- (V. 52) A miraculous event occurs, foreshadowing Jesus' resurrection and the promise of eternal life.

- (V. 53) This foreshadowing verse hints at the coming victory over death.

- (V. 54) Even a Roman soldier, witnessing these extraordinary events, recognizes Jesus' divinity.

- (V. 55-56) The passage acknowledges the faithful women who remained by Jesus' side during his suffering.

- (V. 56) The specific women who remained loyal are named, highlighting their courage and devotion.

- (V. 57) Joseph of Arimathea, a wealthy follower of Jesus, emerges to play a crucial role.

- (V. 58) Joseph, with Pilate's permission, takes possession of Jesus' body for a proper burial.

- (V. 59) Joseph prepares Jesus' body for burial with respect and care.

- (V. 60) Jesus is laid to rest in a new tomb, signifying the hope of new life to come.

- (V. 61) The faithful women remain near the tomb, their presence symbolizing their unwavering devotion.

Prayer: For Gratitude and Hope

Dear God, we thank you for the immeasurable sacrifice of your Son, Jesus Christ. May his love and suffering inspire us to live with faith, hope, and compassion.

The Challenge: Living a Life of Love

This Good Friday, reflect on the significance of Jesus' sacrifice. How can you demonstrate your love and gratitude through your actions?

Interaction

- **The Meaning of the Cross:** Discuss the symbolism of the crucifixion and its impact on humanity's relationship with God.

- **Living a Life of Sacrifice:** Explore the concept of sacrifice and how it can play a role in our daily lives. How can we make choices that prioritize the well-being of others?

Modern Applications: Spreading Love and Hope

The story of the crucifixion offers valuable insights for living a meaningful life:

- **The Power of Love:** Jesus' sacrifice is a testament to the transformative power of love, even in the face of hatred and violence.

- **Living with Faith:** The crucifixion reaffirms the importance of faith in God's plan, even during times of darkness and suffering.

- **Hope for Humanity:** Jesus' death offers hope for redemption and the possibility of a new beginning.

Remember:

Good Friday is a day of somber reflection, but it also lays the groundwork for the celebration of Easter Sunday and the promise of resurrection.

Holy Saturday: A Day of Quiet Contemplation (Matthew 27:62-66)

Reflection: Holding Our Breath

Matthew 27:62-66 offers a brief glimpse into the events following Jesus' crucifixion. This passage portrays a sense of waiting and uncertainty among the characters involved.

Securing the Tomb

- (V. 62) The passage opens with the chief priests and Pharisees approaching Pilate.

- (V. 63) They express concern that Jesus' followers might steal his body and claim he has risen.

- (V. 64) They request that the tomb be guarded to prevent such a scenario.

- (V. 65) Pilate grants their request, allowing them to use their own guards to secure the tomb.

- (V. 66) The chief priests and Pharisees take action to ensure the tomb remains undisturbed.

A Day of Limbo

While this passage focuses on the actions of the religious authorities, it also leaves space to consider the emotions of Jesus' followers. The narrative doesn't explicitly mention the disciples, but we can imagine a sense of grief, confusion, and perhaps even fear gripping them after witnessing Jesus' crucifixion.

Prayer: For Comfort and Hope

Dear God, grant comfort to those who grieve and offer hope in times of uncertainty. Lead us through darkness and towards the light of your promises.

The Challenge: Finding Hope in the Wait

This Holy Saturday, reflect on times in your life when you've had to wait for an answer or endure a period of uncertainty. How can you find hope and trust in God's timing?

Interaction

- **The Power of Waiting:** Discuss the concept of waiting and its role in our spiritual lives. How can periods of waiting strengthen our faith?

- **Hope in the Midst of Uncertainty:** Explore strategies for maintaining hope and trust in God's plan, even when the future seems unclear.

Modern Applications: Finding Peace in Uncertainty

The passage offers valuable insights for navigating challenging times:

- **Facing Uncertainty:** Life is full of uncertainty. Holy Saturday reminds us that even in the absence of clear answers, we can find solace in faith and trust.

- **The Importance of Hope:** Hope is essential for the human spirit. Holy Saturday serves as a reminder that even in darkness, there is always the promise of a new dawn.

Remember:

Holy Saturday is a day of quiet contemplation, a pause before the joyous celebration of Easter Sunday. It's a time to acknowledge the human emotions surrounding Jesus' death while holding onto the hope of resurrection.

NOTES:

Easter Sunday: The Resurrection (Matthew 28:1-10)

Reflection: Victory Over Death

Matthew 28:1-10 recounts the glorious event of Jesus' resurrection. This passage signifies humanity's victory over death and the power of God's love.

The Tomb is Empty

- (V. 1) The passage opens with Mary Magdalene and another Mary approaching the tomb early on Sunday morning.
- (V. 2) A powerful earthquake marks the arrival of an angel, who effortlessly rolls away the heavy stone sealing the tomb.
- (V. 3) The angel's appearance is dazzling and awe-inspiring.
- (V. 4) The guards tasked with securing the tomb are overwhelmed by the angel's presence.

The Angelic Message

- (V. 5-6) The angel reassures the women and proclaims the joyous news of Jesus' resurrection.
- (V. 7) The angel instructs the women to share the news with the disciples, offering a message of hope and reunion.

Encountering the Risen Christ

- (V. 8) The women's emotions are a mixture of fear and overwhelming joy as they race to share the news.
- (V. 9) In a surprising turn of events, Jesus appears to the women on their way.
- (V. 10) Jesus repeats the message for the disciples, emphasizing their future reunion in Galilee.

A New Dawn

The passage ends with a powerful sense of hope and the promise of new beginnings. Jesus' resurrection marks a turning point in history, offering humanity the hope of eternal life.

Prayer: For Renewed Faith and Joy

Dear God, we celebrate the glorious resurrection of your Son, Jesus Christ. May his victory over death fill us with renewed faith and joy.

The Challenge: Living the Resurrection

This Easter Sunday, reflect on how the message of resurrection can influence your daily life. How can you share the hope and joy of Christ's victory with the world?

Interaction

- **The Significance of the Resurrection:** Discuss the importance of Jesus' resurrection in the Christian faith. How does it impact our understanding of life and death?

- **Sharing the Easter Message:** Explore ways to share the message of hope and love associated with Easter Sunday with others in your community.

Modern Applications: Living with Hope

The story of the resurrection offers valuable takeaways for living a meaningful life:

- **Hope in the Face of Challenges:** The resurrection serves as a beacon of hope, reminding us that even in darkness, there is always the promise of light.

- **The Power of Faith:** Faith in God's promises can provide strength and comfort during difficult times.

- **Sharing God's Love:** The Easter message encourages us to share God's love and compassion with the world around us.

Remember:

Easter Sunday is a joyous celebration of Jesus' victory over death. Let the message of hope and love from this passage inspire you to live a life filled with faith and compassion.

Additional Resources:

The Lenten season is a powerful time for reflection and spiritual growth. But how do you carry that momentum forward into the rest of the year? Here's a guide packed with resources to enrich your Lenten practices, find a supportive community, and nurture your faith beyond Easter Sunday.

Lenten Practices and Traditions: A Personalized Journey

Lent isn't a one-size-fits-all experience. Explore different practices to discover what resonates with you:

- **Fasting and Abstinence:** Go beyond just giving up chocolate. Consider a "social media fast" to reconnect with loved ones, or volunteer your time to a cause you care about.

- **Prayer and Reflection:** Carve out quiet time each day for meditation, journaling, or reading inspirational texts.

- **Simple Living:** Declutter your physical and mental space. Practice gratitude for what you have and consider acts of generosity towards others.

- **Daily Devotionals:** Many churches and websites offer daily Lenten readings and reflections delivered straight to your inbox.

- **Faith-Based Podcasts:** Find inspiration and insights on the go with podcasts like "The Bible Project" or "Ask NT Wright Anything."

Finding a Spiritual Community: Where You Belong

A supportive spiritual community can be a lifeline for your faith. Here are some ways to connect:

- **Explore Different Denominations:** Visit different churches or religious institutions to find a place where the teachings and atmosphere resonate with you.

- **Join a Small Group:** Many churches offer small groups focused on Bible study, prayer, or shared interests.

- **Volunteer Opportunities:** Serving others is a powerful way to connect with your faith and like-minded people.

- **Online Faith Communities:** Find online forums or social media groups focused on your specific faith or interests.

Maintaining Your Faith Beyond Lent: Everyday Inspiration

Lent may be over, but your faith journey continues! Here are some tips to keep your faith vibrant:

- **Integrate Daily Rituals:** Develop a consistent prayer or meditation practice that fits your schedule.

- **Faith-Based Books and Movies:** Seek out inspirational literature, documentaries, or movies that uplift your spirit.

- **Nature as a Spiritual Guide:** Take time for walks in nature, appreciating the beauty and wonder of creation.

- **Practice Gratitude:** Reflect on the blessings in your life, big and small. You can even keep a gratitude journal.

- **Faith-Based Service:** Find a cause you care about and volunteer regularly. Helping others strengthens your faith and connection to the community.

Remember: Your faith journey is unique. Explore, experiment, and find what nourishes your spirit. These resources are just a starting point – embrace the adventure of a life filled with faith!

Closing Prayer

Almighty God, as we close this chapter in our Lenten journey with Jesus, we give thanks for the graces received and the lessons learned. May the reflections we encountered illuminate our path and strengthen our resolve to follow Your will. Grant us the courage to continue carrying our crosses, the perseverance to overcome temptation, and the unwavering faith to reach the glorious light of Easter. We pray for the continued strength to embody Your love and compassion in all we do.

In Jesus' holy name, Amen.

Printed in Great Britain
by Amazon